THE OLD TESTAMENT
AGAINST ITS
ENVIRONMENT

STUDIES IN BIBLICAL THEOLOGY

A series of monographs designed to provide clergy and laymen with the best work in biblical scholarship both in this country and abroad.

STUDIES IN BIBLICAL THEOLOGY · 2

THE OLD TESTAMENT AGAINST ITS ENVIRONMENT

G. ERNEST WRIGHT

SCM PRESS LTD
BLOOMSBURY STREET LONDON

SBN 334 01161 2

First published December 1950
Reprinted August 1951
Reprinted January 1953
Reprinted June 1954
Reprinted May 1955
Reprinted August 1957
Reprinted August 1960
Reprinted December 1962
Reprinted May 1966
Reprinted March 1968

Printed in Great Britain by
Northumberland Press Limited
Gateshead on Tyne

CONTENTS

Foreword 7

I 'WHAT GREAT NATION HATH A GOD LIKE THE LORD?' 9

I. The limitations of the metaphor of growth as an explanation of religious phenomena in the Bible. II. The theological nature of polytheism. III. The Israelite mutation or radical break with the current theologies. IV. The problem of defining Israelite monotheism.

II 'HE ESTABLISHED A TESTIMONY IN ISRAEL' 42

I. The tension in Israel between the revealed and actual orders of society. II. The importance of the doctrine of election for the understanding of the Old Testament. III. Covenant or legal compact as the terminology in which the meaning of election was expressed. IV. The covenant at Sinai in relation to the theology of kingship in polytheism and in Israel. V. The interpretation of life and the meaning of history. VI. Biblical faith as revealed religion in contrast to natural or cultural religion.

III 'WHAT DOTH THE LORD THY GOD REQUIRE?' 77

I. Israel's struggle against polytheistic magic, divination, and demons. II. The nature of religious festivals in polytheism and in Israel. III. The sacrificial cultus in polytheism and in Israel.

Index 113

FOREWORD

THIS MONOGRAPH is an expanded edition of Part I of the Haskell Lectures, presented at the Oberlin Graduate School of Theology in April, 1949; Part II was given by my colleague, Professor Floyd V. Filson. The theme of the Lectures is 'The Bible Against Its Environment,' and the two Parts attempt a treatment of the same three subjects in the Old and New Testaments respectively. These subjects are the nature of God, the meaning of life and history, and the worship and service of God.

The purpose of the lectures is to examine and lay emphasis upon those central elements of Biblical faith which are so unique and *sui generis* that they cannot have developed by any natural evolutionary process from the pagan world in which they appeared. They cannot be explained, therefore, by environmental or geographical conditioning. The argument is thus directed against the extreme positions taken by those scholars, who, absorbed in the study of ancient civilization and comparative religion, have sought to explain and expound Biblical faith primarily in developmental terms. It is the contention of this monograph that the faith of Israel even in its earliest and basic forms is so utterly different from that of the contemporary polytheisms that one simply cannot explain it fully by evolutionary or environmental categories. Such a contention runs somewhat counter to the habits of thought and the methodological assumptions of many leading scholars of the last two generations. Yet it is difficult to see how any other conclusion is justified by the facts as we now know them from the vast accumulation of knowledge about the Biblical world.

I should like to express my indebtedness to Professor W. F. Albright of Johns Hopkins University for numerous suggestions and indeed for the general point of view here maintained, to Professor Thorkild Jacobsen of the Oriental Institute of the University of Chicago for his stimulating lectures on Mesopotamian religion in a seminar which he permitted me to attend, and to Dean Leonard A. Stidley and the faculty of the Oberlin Graduate School of Theology for the opportunity of presenting the lectures and for the kind hospitality accorded me on their campus.

G. E. W.

Sept. 19, 1949.

ACKNOWLEDGMENTS

Grateful acknowledgment is made to the following publishers for permission to quote from books published by them: to the Clarendon Press for a quotation from H. Wheeler Robinson, *Inspiration and Revelation in the Old Testament*, p. 241; to Columbia University Press for quotations from H. Frankfort, *Ancient Egyptian Religion*, pp. 73 and 77; to the Johns Hopkins Press for a quotation from W. F. Albright, *Archaeology and the Religion of Israel*, p. 116; to the Macmillan Company for a quotation from Harry Emerson Fosdick, *The Modern Use of the Bible*, pp. 11-12; to the Oxford University Press for a quotation from Rudolph Otto, *The Idea of the Holy*, pp. 3-4; to the same Press and to Povl Branner of Copenhagen for a quotation from J. Pederson, *Israel III-IV*, p. 662; and to the University of Chicago Press for quotations from H. Frankfort, *et al.*, *The Intellectual Adventure of Ancient Man*, pp. 199, 363, 371, 373, and from H. Frankfort, *Kingship and the Gods*, pp. 278, 279, 341-2.

CHAPTER ONE

'WHAT GREAT NATION HATH A GOD LIKE THE LORD?'

I

TO WHAT extent can the metaphor of growth be used to explain what happened in history? Specifically, how valid is it as an explanation of the significance of the Old Testament? By the nineteenth century the idea of progress had taken such a powerful hold upon men's minds that it was very naturally applied to the Bible. The Scripture now began to appear as the record of a 'progressive revelation,' though generally described in terms of man's gradual growth in the apprehension of the Divine. The real meaning of the Old Testament was explained by means of the metaphor of growth, derived from biology. In the Bible, it is now asserted, we can see the development from seed, to plant, to fruit, or from babe, to youth, to full-grown maturity, or from the primitive, to the developed, to the culmination. In the words of Harry Emerson Fosdick: 'No longer can we think of the Book as on a level, no longer read its maturer passages back into its earlier sources. We know now that every idea in the Bible started from primitive and childlike origins and, with however many setbacks and delays, grew in scope and height toward the culmination in Christ's gospel. We know now that the Bible is the record of an amazing spiritual development.'[1] In such a point of view it is inevitable that the study of theology, the examination of the faith by which and in which a people live, should become subservient to history. As a result Biblical theology and the history of Biblical religion actually came to be conceived as one and the same thing.[2] Historical evolution

[1] *The Modern Use of the Bible* (New York, 1924), pp. 11 f.

[2] For an excellent review of the manner in which this came about in the Old Testament field of study, see James D. Smart, 'The Death and

claimed the right of way over everything which stood in its path.

Like all metaphors this one of growth has both its good and its bad applications. On the one hand, it calls attention to the fact that the Bible is primarily a history covering some two thousand years. Consequently, one cannot examine it through the spectacles of a static conception of time. One cannot expect to find the theology of Paul in the Books of Kings or that of Second Isaiah in the Song of Deborah. On the other hand, however, the metaphor of growth has so pervaded our minds that in both theology and comparative religion we have tended to assume that the gradual evolution of rational concepts is the main problem of our enquiry. Our minds are thus focused upon the discovery of those primitive ideas and notions of lower value from which the higher values could have evolved.[3] In the study of the Bible, therefore, we tend to assume that the earlier our literary source material, the more primitive should be its religious teaching and the nearer it should stand to the pagan environment in which it arose. Consequently, it is not uncommon to describe the early literature of Israel by means of the lowest theological common denominator. The anthropomorphism of the Adam and Eve story, for example, must be primitive and we are entitled to read into it all sorts of crude notions simply because we must make room for growth and development. The story of Jacob's wrestling with the angel in Gen. 32.24 ff. betrays its primitive origin, and thus 'can be regarded only as a piece of chauvinistic patriotism proving to the Israelite that eventually his nation would prevail over all others in spite of the dark night through which they had to suffer.'[4]

Rebirth of Old Testament Theology,' *Journal of Religion,* Vol. XXIII (1943), pp. 1-11, 125-36.

[3] Cf. Rudolf Otto, *The Idea of the Holy* (London, 1931), pp. 3-4.

[4] C. C. McCown, *Journal of Biblical Literature,* Vol. LXIII (1944), pp. 332 f. Cf. John Skinner, *A Critical and Exegetical Commentary on Genesis* (London, New York, revised ed. 1925), pp. 411 f. Contrast S. R. Driver, *The Book of Genesis* (London, New York, 1904), pp. 296 f.; and even H. Gunkel, *Genesis* (Göttingen, 1901), pp. 328 ff.

The so-called 'ritual decalogue' supposed to exist in Ex. 34 does not deal with morality, so it must be older in origin than the 'ethical' decalogue in Ex. 20.

The application of the metaphor of growth to the study of the Bible, therefore, has produced not only a new and more healthy attitude toward the study of Biblical history; it has also generated a habit of mind which easily misinterprets the subject matter because it must always evaluate in terms of an ascending scale of values. A major question, then, which confronts the Biblical interpreter to-day has a twofold aspect: does the metaphor of growth focus attention on the primary problem of Biblical enquiry; and, if not, in what way can it be used?

As a device for understanding the Bible, the idea of development lays emphasis inevitably upon the process of human discovery rather than on revelation, on gradual evolution rather than on mutation. Yet both are factors to be dealt with in Biblical history, and the one can hardly be set aside in favor of the other. The living God, says the Bible, breaks into a people's life and by mighty acts performs his wonders in their behalf. The people see, hear, understand, obey, rebel. In so doing they discover ever more clearly the meaning of their election and of the purpose of God. This 'challenge-and-response' nature of the Biblical point of view cannot easily be accommodated to a single metaphor such as growth. Yet scholars have busied themselves in the attempt, with a result that is at the same moment both valid and misleading: valid in so far, for example, as the effort has led to the accumulation of a tremendous amount of facts and information without which the progress of Biblical history cannot be understood; misleading in so far as these facts are assumed to explain all phenomena within the Bible and indeed the Bible itself.

The work of archaeology in its attempt to re-create the Biblical environment has been of particular importance. No longer does the Bible project 'from the chaos of prehistory . . . as though it were a monstrous fossil, with no contemporary evidence to demonstrate its authenticity and its origin.'[5] Yet how far can the study of the environment of Israel, for example, be used to explain the faith of Israel? Specifically, has the God of Israel evolved from the gods of the nations, or Israelite monotheism from pagan polytheism?

During the past century our preoccupation with the idea of development has led us to answer this last question in the affirmative. The patriarchal narratives have been deciphered in such a way as to reveal an animism or polydemonism. The nature of this religion was assumed to be explained by the type of comparative material collected by Sir James Frazer in his *Golden Bough*. From animism Israel was thought to have evolved through polytheism and henotheism to monotheism. Israel and her environment were understood to coalesce in large measure before the days of the prophets; only gradually thereafter did she free herself from its influence.[6] Environment and growth are here used as the chief clues for the understanding of the real meaning of Israel's achievement. Are they sufficient, or has the measure of truth which they contain blinded us to other factors which they cannot explain?

In the first place, it is increasingly realized to-day that the attempt to make of the Old Testament a source book for the evolution of religion from very primitive to highly advanced concepts has been made possible only by means of a radical misinterpretation of the literature. In the history of Israel as in the history of other peoples there are numerous primitive

[5] W. F. Albright, 'Recent Discoveries in Bible Lands,' Supplement to Robert Young, *Analytical Concordance* (New York, 1936), p. 1.

[6] For a convenient exposition of this point of view, see W. O. E. Oesterley and T. H. Robinson, *Hebrew Religion: Its Origin and Development* (New York, 1st ed., 1930). One fourth of this book is given over to the description of the animistic and magical background of Israel's religion. Yet we now know that in doing this, the authors are dealing neither with Patriarchal nor with pagan religion of the day, but chiefly with Stone Age survivals and relics, the true meaning of which either in Israel or in contemporary polytheism is scarcely understood.

survivals. Is it possible to construct a system out of them in Israel and thus presume that we have defined early Hebrew religion? One cannot do this, we now know, with the contemporary polytheisms of Egypt, Canaan, or Babylon, nor for any known religion of the ancient world.[7] Doubt must therefore be thrown on any picture of the God of Israel which attempts to portray him as a purely localized, anthropomorphic, nature deity, limited to tribe, shrine, or mountain, pacified by human sacrifice, a crude, capricious little despot whose hate and cruelty are unlimited by any moral consistency of character. It would be very difficult to find a parallel to such a god among any of the gods of the time. One must therefore become suspicious of the methodology which claims to discover such a deity, and to examine more carefully the modifying and contrary evidences in the oldest narratives and collections of law.

In the second place, we cannot assume that a mere description of an evolutionary process provides the explanation for matters which belong to the realm of religious faith. The development of ideas is not a theme in which Biblical writers show much interest, nor is it one which can create a community of faith, a people of God. How did Israel become a nation with such faith in its God that its very existence was conceived to be a miracle of grace? The prophets did not invent this remarkable conception since it existed before them. Sociological study cannot explain it, since the change in material status from nomadic to agricultural life could effect no such religious innovation. Nor can the environment provide the answer, since the Old Testament bears eloquent witness to the fact that Canaanite religion was the most dangerous and disintegrative factor which the faith of Israel had to face.[8] Israel's knowledge

[7] For an up-to-date review of the theologies of Egypt and Babylon at this time, see now Frankfort, Frankfort, Wilson, Jacobsen, and Irwin, *The Intellectual Adventure of Ancient Man* (Chicago, 1946).

[8] At one time it was maintained that monotheism naturally arose in Arabia because of the monotony, uniformity, and austerity of desert life (see Ernest Renan, *History of the People of Israel,* Vol. I, Boston, 1888,

of her election by God must be traced to a theological reflection on the meaning of the Exodus from Egypt. It is a primary datum in Old Testament theology, and it belongs to a realm of religious faith which cannot be described or understood by the criteria of growth.[9]

This leads us to a third consideration, derived from an argument of Rudolf Otto in his book, *The Idea of the Holy*:[10]

> There is something presupposed by history as such . . . which alone makes it history, and that is the existence of a *quale*, something with a potentiality of its own, capable of *becoming*, in the special sense of coming to be that to which it was predisposed and predetermined. . . . We only have the history of a people in proportion as it enters upon its course equipped with an endowment of talents and tendencies; it must already *be something* if it is really to become anything. And biography is a lamentable and unreal business in the case of a man who has no real unique potentiality of his own, no special idiosyncrasy, and is therefore a mere point of intersection for various fortuitous causal series, acted on, as it were, from without. Biography is only a real narration of real life where, by the interplay of stimulus and experience on the one side and predisposition and natural endowment on the other, something individual and unique comes into being, which is therefore neither the result of a 'mere self-unfolding' nor yet the sum of mere traces and impressions, written from without from moment to moment upon a 'tabula rasa.'

What was this *something* in early Israel which predisposed

Chap. IV). This idea has never commended itself, however, because the Arabs were typical polytheists before the days of Mohammed. Geography may explain some of the conditioning of revelation, but it cannot provide a substitute or explanation for the phenomenon itself.

[9] For an excellent and succinct critique of the evolutionary approach to the Old Testament, see W. Eichrodt's review of H. E. Fosdick, *Guide to the Understanding of the Bible* in *Journal of Biblical Literature*, Vol. LXV (1946), pp. 205 ff. Many similar references could be given, especially from German scholars, who reacted earlier against the older views than did the scholars of England and America; cf. H. Gressmann, *Mose und seine Zeit* (Göttingen, 1913). The classic attack on the assumption that the phenomena of religion, composed so largely of the 'non-rational' and the 'numinous,' can be understood merely by intellectual criteria is, of course, the work of Rudolf Otto, referred to in Note 3.

[10] p. 180.

and predetermined the course of Biblical history? What is the Israelite mutation,[11] which made the particular and peculiar evolution of Biblical faith a possibility? This is precisely what the study of environment and development has been unable to define. It has been assumed that a considerable proportion of Israel's allegedly unique contributions to religion were not of her own discovery. She borrowed from many sources, and her uniqueness consisted in the alterations and improvements which she imposed upon what was borrowed.[12] But what led to these 'alterations' and 'improvements'? Why is this question not examined? I find it necessary to agree with W. Eichrodt when he says that the source of the difficulty lies in the inability of the developmental hypothesis to take seriously the story of God's revelation and covenant at Mt. Sinai. Thus no fixed starting point is provided for the unfolding of Israel's knowledge of God. Even Wellhausen, the great pathfinder of the developmental history, often used to admit: 'Why Chemosh of Moab never became the God of righteousness and the Creator of heaven and earth, is a question to which one can give no satisfactory answer.' The great historian of antiquity, Edward Meyer, pointed out the futility of seeking an explanation in a theory of Moses' elevation of an old nature deity to a tribal god. The phrase with which the work of Moses is often described, 'Yahweh God of Israel and Israel people of Yahweh,' is a cliché without real content which *mutatis mutandis* could also be used for other folk-religions.[13]

[11] 'Epigenesis' is perhaps a much better word than 'mutation,' but the latter is used throughout this chapter because its general meaning is more widely understood. What is meant is a radical revolution, as opposed to evolution, which is not entirely explainable by the empirical data.

[12] So, for example, most recently C. C. McCown, 'Geographical Conditioning of Religious Experience in Palestine,' in H. R. Willoughby, ed., *The Study of the Bible To-day and To-morrow* (Chicago, 1947), pp. 240 ff.

[13] See Eichrodt, op. cit., pp. 211 f., and Meyer, *Die Israeliten und ihre Nachbarstämme* (Halle, 1906), p. 451, n.1.

It seems to me that the only avenue of approach toward a solution of our problem is through a consideration of those primary elements of Israel's faith which distinguish it sharply from the religions of its environment. The dangers of such a procedure are obvious. We must not turn our backs upon the fruits of historical and critical study nor upon the manifold evidences of development in the Israelite religious consciousness. Yet religious faith is more than a series of rationally developed doctrines. It is an inclusive interpretation of life which gives meaning to existence; it implies an Object, a 'Wholly Other,' to which one is committed by ties of conviction and trust, and which supplies the answer to the question: 'Why do I live, and how am I to live, that my hope and my effort may have meaning?' Every religion has its primary concern at this point. Each has its own analysis of and answer to the problem of life. How did the answer of Israel differ from that of her neighbors?

II

At the outset it is necessary to discuss the nature of the *Object* of faith. The treatment of necessity must be brief and schematic, but the nature of the deity worshipped is the basic consideration upon which all other considerations rest.

Long before the history of Israel began, the ancient Near East had left any stage of animism or dynamism far behind. The first temples are known to have been in existence long before 4000 B.C.[14] When the historical period proper begins during the third millennium, Egypt, Mesopotamia, and presumably Palestine-Syria possessed a highly developed polytheism. The forces and powers of the universe had been distinguished and

[14] In Mesopotamia the earliest temples found are those of the Obeid period (*ca.* end of the fifth or beginning of fourth millennium B.C.) at Tepe Gawra in the north and at Eridu in the south. At Jericho in Palestine a still earlier temple has been found, dating from the Neolithic period.

the category of personality applied to them. They could thus be known and understood. They could be met and worshipped in their temples, which were conceived as great manor houses or palaces where the gods lived and were cared for by their servants.[15] The powers of the great gods were cosmic in extent; their limitations were not conceived geographically or ethnically. Each religion comprehended the universe, and the gods were limited only by their own inner natures and by the order of the cosmos they themselves had established.

How had men come to know and to identify them? It was not by rational analysis, but by the experience of power and force in nature as encountered in the struggle for existence. The polytheist saw the problem of his life over against the powers of nature which he could not control but on which he was utterly dependent. The awesome power of a great thunderstorm, the majestic expanse and depth of the heavens, the mysterious brilliance of the moon and the stars, the wonderful blessing of the sun's warmth, the miraculous fecundity of the earth, the terrible reality of death, all these and many more awakened in him feelings of awe and wonder. He did not distinguish between reality and the force in or behind it. In the storm he meets the God Storm. Nature is alive, and its powers are distinguished as personal because man has directly experienced them. There is no such thing as the inanimate. Man lives in the realm of a throbbing, personal nature, the kingdom of the holy gods. He is caught in the interplay of gigantic forces to which he must integrate his life. They are known to him because he has experienced them, not as objects, but as personalities so much greater in power than his own that of necessity he worships and serves them.

[15] Cf. Thorkild Jacobsen, 'Temples, Mesopotamian,' in Vergilius Ferm, ed., *Encyclopedia of Religion* (New York, 1945), pp. 770 f.; and the symposium by Harold H. Nelson, A. Leo Oppenheim, G. Ernest Wright, and Floyd V. Filson, 'The Significance of the Temple in the Ancient Near East,' *Biblical Archaeologist,* Vol. VII (1944), Nos. 3 and 4.

The number of these gods thus identified was tremendous; in Mesopotamia that number was in the thousands. Yet nature is not chaotic; it has a rhythm and order which for the most part can be depended upon. The plurality of nature is thus regulated; the gods have organized the universe into a cosmic state, in which each power has a specific role to play. This universal order 'did not appear as something given; rather it became something achieved—achieved through a continual integration of the many cosmic wills.'[16] In Mesopotamia all authority lay within the personality of the Sky, Anu; but it was a passive authority. Executive force was wielded originally by the Storm, Enlil, who had been selected as king of the gods. Decisions were made by the cosmic assembly, and it was the duty of the king to carry them out. In Canaan there existed a similar arrangement. The authoritarian head of the pantheon was El, but the chief executive, the king, was the personified Storm, Hadad, the Baal or Lord of the gods and men.

Complementary powers were paired as male and female. Each god had his goddess, and their children were likewise members of the cosmic order. Each of the great gods had his household of servants and attendants. Yet as nature is not always peaceful and orderly, neither was the kingdom of the gods. Many of them, like the forces of nature which they were, had hidden depths in their personalities, energies which could occasion every sort of immorality and tragedy. At one and the same time they were just and chaotic, orderly and destructive. Thus Storm as divine king was the executive power of the cosmic order, but at times he was wilful, fickle, and destructive. Ordinarily he possessed a consistency of character, but his primitive background as natural force led him to commit acts which on occasion other gods must nullify or seek to modify. As personalities who were increasingly socialized and responsible for the growing complexity of civilized life, few of the gods were ever able completely to shake off those hidden depths of

[16] Thorkild Jacobsen in *Intellectual Adventure of Ancient Man*, p. 127.

violence inherent in the non-moral nature in which they arose. Some of the chief opposing forces of nature, however, were not seen as occasioned by one personality, but by a conflict of personalities. The most notable illustration of this was the opposition of life and death, particularly the fertility of nature in the spring as opposed by the death of the summer's drought. The god who produced this fertility in earth was killed each year by the forces of death, and revived each fall by the magic of his wife and the beneficent Sun.

In describing the cosmology and operation of the universe the polytheist used the only language which was natural to his personal conception of the world. That was the language of myth. He thought, not in terms of an abstract logic, but in terms of what has aptly been called 'mythopoetry.'[17] He was not concerned with the abstract, systematic use of his reason; he experienced divine acts and events in which his own life and death were directly involved. His religious literature, therefore, was his witness to his experience with divine personalities and to his reflection on what that experience meant. To us his mythopoeic stories about the gods have an unreal, other-worldly character, with so little direct concern with his own life. The modern religious individualist, who searches so diligently for spiritual light and power, would find little here to satisfy him. Yet myth to the polytheist was the cloak of authoritative truth, in the yearly re-enactment of which he identified himself with its leading powers and thus secured the integration of his social existence with the activity of nature. Mythopoetry was thus not a mere form of entertainment, nor was it a mere explanation of matters which troubled the intellect; it was the narration in story form of the universal facts of life to which man must adjust himself.

[17] So the authors of the volume cited in notes 7 and 16, to which the writer is heavily indebted in this section.

III

When we turn to the Old Testament, a literature produced in the midst of that polytheistic world, we immediately find ourselves in a totally different religious atmosphere where different answers have been given to man's basic questioning.

An expert on ancient polytheism, Professor Henri Frankfort, sought to learn how it was that the mythopoeic mode of thinking came to be broken in that ancient world. He turned to the early Greek philosophers and to the records of Israel, and concluded that the one was as radical a departure from the old ways as was the other. He sets down his impressions of the Old Testament as follows:[18]

> When we read in Psalm 19 that 'the heavens declare the glory of God; and the firmament sheweth his handiwork,' we hear a voice which mocks the beliefs of Egyptians and Babylonians. The heavens, which were to the psalmist but a witness of God's greatness, were to the Mesopotamians the very majesty of godhead, the highest ruler, Anu. To the Egyptians the heavens signified the mystery of the divine mother through whom man was reborn. In Egypt and Mesopotamia the divine was comprehended as immanent: the gods were in nature. The Egyptians saw in the sun all that a man may know of the Creator; the Mesopotamians viewed the sun as the god Shamash, the guarantor of justice. But to the psalmist the sun was God's devoted servant who is as a bridegroom coming out of his chamber, and 'rejoiceth as a strong man to run a race.' The God of the psalmists and the prophets was not in nature. He transcended nature—and transcended, likewise, the realm of mythopoeic thought. It would seem that the Hebrews, no less than the Greeks, broke with the mode of speculation which had prevailed up to their time.

It is important to recognize, however, that this Hebrew achievement was not the product of purely speculative thought any more than was the analysis of the divine among polytheists. The power of Yahweh the God of Israel was known because he had chosen this people for himself, because he had humbled Pharaoh and delivered Israel from slavery, had formed a dis-

[18] *Ibid.*, p. 363.

pirited people into a nation and given them a law and an 'inheritance' of land. Israel had been in bondage, but was now freed. No abstract words were needed to describe God's being; it was sufficient to identify him with a simple historical statement: he was the God who had brought Israel out of the land of Egypt, out of the house of bondage (Ex. 20.2).

Such was the God whom Israel knew. Wherever the people were or in whatever circumstance, they encountered and acknowledged the power of the God who had delivered them. Looking back to the days of their fathers, they recognized his gracious providence in revealing himself to Abraham, Isaac, and Jacob, even though under a different name or epithets. In Egypt he saw their affliction and visited them. At Mt. Sinai or Horeb and again in battle with Sisera, he was recognized in the phenomena of a storm.[19] Metaphors which were applied to the pagan gods of the storm could also be applied to him, for lightning was his arrow and thunder his voice. Like Baal of Canaan he could be described in poetry as riding on a cherub or a cloud-enveloped chariot, uttering peals of thunder and sending out his darts of lightning. Even an epithet of Baal, 'the rider of the clouds,' could be used of him.[20] When Israel had adjusted to

[19] Ex. 19.16-19 and Judg. 5. The repeated attempts to interpret the theophany on Mt. Sinai as inferring a volcanic disturbance (from which it is also inferred that Mt. Sinai must be in Arabia) have little to commend them. I must agree with a remark of Johs. Pedersen in *Israel: its Life and Culture* III-IV (London, 1940), p. 662: 'A search might with equal justice be instituted for the mountains that melted like wax when Yahweh passed over the hills of the earth. The author has done all that he could to convey an idea of the might of Yahweh. The dark cloud, the thunder and lightning, the trumpet blast, the smoke, are all meant to express Yahweh's power over the world of nature. He causes noise and revolutions when he touches it, as we know from numerous descriptions of Yahweh's procedure.'

[20] See Deut. 33.26; Ps. 68.4, 33; Isa. 19.1. Note especially also 2 Sam. 22—Ps. 18; both this and Ps. 68 have been borrowed in part from Canaan and used as hymns of praise for Yahweh. For the phrase 'rider of the clouds' in the Ugaritic literature see word 1869 in Cyrus H. Gordon, *Ugaritic Handbook*, Vol. III (Rome, 1947).

agricultural life Yahweh was recognized as the power in earth's fertility, the one who 'maketh the hinds to calve' (Ps. 29.9),[21] the author of the blessings of heaven (rain), of the deep (springs), of breast and womb (Gen. 49.25; cf. Deut. 33.13 ff.)—functions earlier ascribed in similar terms to the Canaanite Baal. Yet Yahweh was no mere storm or fertility deity. Even in the early poetry which we have just been quoting, he is the great Lord whose 'righteous' acts in Israel's behalf men shall rehearse (Judg. 5.11). One poet exclaims: 'Happy art thou, O Israel; who is like unto thee—a people saved by Yahweh!' (Deut. 33.29).

The Israelite knowledge of God, therefore, was not founded in the first instance on the numinous awareness of nature, as was the case in polytheism. It was based on historical event. In polytheism the original and basic metaphors through which the divine was apprehended can be shown to have been derived from nature; metaphors drawn from society, such as lord, king, judge, craftsman, mother, and the like, while central in the historical period, have none the less been imposed on the earlier forms. In Israel the exact opposite is the case. Metaphors from nature, for the most part borrowed from Canaanite religion, were not the basic language by which God who had revealed himself through historical events could be described or apprehended. That the God of Israel could also be depicted as Lord of nature by means of borrowed terms indicates only his power. So great was he that the Israelite acknowledged his Lordship over every phenomenon that his experience encountered.[22] No

[21] It is now recognized that Ps. 29 was in its original form a hymn to Baal, the storm and fertility god of Canaan, and was borrowed by Israel with appropriate changes. This phrase once described a characteristic power of Baal, but it is now used of Yahweh, God of Israel. See H. L. Ginsberg, *Biblical Archaeologist,* Vol. VIII (1945), No. 2, pp. 53 f.

[22] For the primary nature of the metaphors 'lord' and 'king' in Israelite faith, metaphors on which most of the Old Testament religious vocabulary is based, see the writer, 'The Terminology of Old Testament Religion and its Significance,' *Journal of Near Eastern Studies*, Vol. I (1942), pp. 404 ff. The conclusions are summarized in more popular

one aspect of nature was more characteristic of Yahweh than another; he was Lord both of the natural and the historical event, 'the God of heaven and the God of the earth' (Gen. 24.3). He therefore transcended nature, as he transcended history.

It was not that Israelite leaders necessarily reasoned all this out in a speculative way. The experience of their people led them to know it almost intuitively. They recognized their God in the first instance as authoritative and decisive power. And the point where that power was apprehended led them to an entirely different faith from that of the polytheist. The problem of life was seen, not as an integration with the forces of nature, but as an adjustment to the will of the God who had chosen them.

Other aspects of Israel's God are even more astonishing than those just described. For some reason, perhaps in part because of the historical nature of God's revelation, the Israelite did not combine the complementary forces of nature by means of a duality expressed in terms of sex. While the category of personality is, of course, applied to Yahweh and while the pronouns used are in their masculine gender, there is no complementary feminine. The duality of male and female is to be found only in the created world; it is not a part of the Godhead, which is essentially sexless. Biblical Hebrew has no word for goddess. Equally phenomenal is the preservation of God's mystery and holiness by the prohibition of images, either of God himself or of any other spiritual being in heaven or on earth, a prohibition preserved in the oldest law which the Old Testament contains.[23]

At this point it is important that distinctions be made between the 'official' doctrines of the faith and the actual practices of

form in the writer's *Challenge of Israel's Faith* (Chicago, 1944, London, 1946), Chap. III.

[23] Ex. 20.4—Deut. 5.8; Ex. 20.23 (E), 34.17 (J). The commandment is thus preserved in both the J and the E documents.

the common people. There is no image of deity ever mentioned in Patriarchal worship,[24] nor in connection with the institution of the Tabernacle which served as the central shrine of the tribal amphictyony,[25] nor in the Temple of Solomon.[26] On the other hand, we know from archaeology that Israelites possessed small plaques or figurines of the Canaanite fertility and mother goddesses in great number.[27] This indicates the widespread syncretism which went on in early Israel, precisely as the literature frankly testifies. When the Aramaeans and Philistines settled in Canaanite territory, they adopted Canaanite customs. When the Amorites settled in Mesopotamia, they took over Sumerian religion, adjusting their own religious pantheon to it. Similarly, the people of Israel were tempted to adopt the customs of their environment. Yet in the vast mass of debris dug out of Israelite towns there is yet to be found an image of a male deity. This is a surprising fact, and future work may discover such objects. Nevertheless the evidence is

[24] The E document implies that this religious innovation was indeed Patriarchal. The family of Laban had household idols or teraphim which Rachel stole, perhaps not so much for religious reasons as to insure inheritance rights for Jacob (Gen. 31.19, 30; see C. H. Gordon, *Biblical Archaeologist*, Vol. III (1940), No.1, p. 6). When the family arrived in Canaan, they were told to put away these 'foreign gods' in their midst and to purify themselves and change their garments (Gen. 35.2, 4).

[25] The historical importance of the early tribal amphictyony with its central shrine or Tabernacle can no longer be denied: see M. Noth, *Das System der zwölf Stämme Israels* (Stuttgart, 1930); A. Alt, *Die Staatenbildung der Israeliten in Palästina* (Leipzig, 1930): Frank M. Cross, Jr., 'The Tabernacle', *Biblical Archaeologist*, Vol. X (1947), No. 3.

[26] On this general subject see the judicious discussion of S. R. Driver, *The Book of Exodus* (Cambridge, 1911), pp. 415 f. An exception to the general statement may be the 'Brazen Serpent,' erected by Moses on a pole in the wilderness to save those who looked upon it from a plague (Num. 21.8-9), which was preserved in the Temple. People evidently came to worship it as an idol and Hezekiah had it broken into pieces (2 Kings 18.4).

[27] See James B. Pritchard, *Palestinian Figurines in Relation to Certain Goddesses Known Through Literature* (New Haven, 1943).

vividly clear that the prohibition against images of Yahweh was so deeply fixed in early Israel, that even the unenlightened and the tolerant understood that Yahweh was simply not to be honored in this way. While other practices might be borrowed, this was not one of them.[28] God was not to be seen or touched by human hands. His holiness and mystery were too great to allow any presumption or undue familiarity of approach. Theophany in the Old Testament is always pictured in terms likely to arouse awe, wonder, and reverence. Outside of Genesis the appearance of God is always accompanied by his glory, the refulgent cloud or smoke which hid his being, for no person can see him and live (Ex. 33.20).

It is true that Yahweh was portrayed frankly and openly in an anthropomorphic manner. Yet here again a distinction over against polytheism must be made. While the gods of the latter are dominantly anthropomorphic in the historical period, their connection with the natural world is emphasized by the use of other metaphors than the personal. In Egypt this is especially clear, for there almost every animal and bird of the land could be used to represent deity. In Canaan and Babylon the same tendency was present to a lesser degree. The bull of heaven was a metaphor commonly used for El and Baal in Canaan and for Anu and Enlil, among others, in Mesopotamia. The bird, the snake, the fish, and all sorts of hybrid forms were also used. In the world of demons and lesser deities composite creatures appear in profusion. While the inner structure of all the gods, including that of the dragons of chaos, Tiamat and Leviathan, was personal, with the result that they could be approached by human beings, there was little stability in the conception of the outward form of the gods, primarily because the worlds of nature, society and the supernatural were not sharply distinguished. All three were part of the integrated cosmos, and each

[28] Cf. the writer in *Biblical Archaeologist,* Vol. VI (1943), No. 1, p. 16. See further W. F. Albright, *Archaeology and the Religion of Israel* (Baltimore, 1942), pp. 110 ff.

was embedded in the other.[29] In the Old Testament, however, a fundamental kinship exists between God and man which exists between God and no other creature of earth. There can be no confusion of metaphors, therefore, in describing him. The Israelite language in depicting the divine is almost solely drawn from the categories of personality and society; indeed this is the basic language of the Bible and of the Jewish and Christian religion.[30]

One further observation alone can be made here. That is the remarkable fact that the God of Israel has no mythology. Since history rather than nature was the *primary* sphere of his revelation, Israel's effort was to tell the story of her past in terms of God's activity. There was no necessity for nature myths. Yahweh, for example, was no dying-rising God like Baal of Canaan. He was *the living God*. This phrase, used again and again so triumphantly, was a challenge to Canaanite conceptions. In the form *hay Yahweh,* 'As Yahweh liveth,' it was

[29] This point is made especially clear by the authors of *The Intellectual Adventure of Ancient Man*. See also H. Frankfort, *Kingship and the Gods* (Chicago, 1948), Chap. 1; and *Ancient Egyptian Religion* (New York, 1948), Chap. 1.

[30] See further the writer's remarks in *Challenge of Israel's Faith,* pp. 65 ff.; and especially the excellent article of J. Hempel, 'Die Grenzen des Anthropomorphismus Jahwes im Alten Testament,' *Zeitschrift für die Alttestamentliche Wissenschaft*, Vol. 57 (1939), pp. 75 ff. The golden calf (bull) which Aaron made (Ex. 32) and those erected by Jeroboam at Bethel and Dan (1 Kings 12.28-29) appear at first glance to be exceptions to the anthropomorphism of Yahweh. Yet Hempel (*ibid.*), H. Th. Obbink (*Zeitschrift f.d. A. T. Wissenschaft,* Vol. 47, 1929, pp. 264 ff.), A. Alt (*Reallexikon der Vorgeschichte*, Vol. VI, 1926, p. 148), and Albright (*From the Stone Age to Christianity,* Baltimore, 1940, pp. 228 ff.), are certainly correct in their view, based on a multitude of archaeological parallels, that these animals were originally intended as pedestals for the invisible deity, similar in function to the cherubim of the Solomonic temple. The chief difference, in my view, was that the cherubim were hidden away in the holy of holies of the Temple, whereas the bulls of Jeroboam were open to public view with the result that many began to worship them as idols. This would account for the strong prophetic polemic against them.

the primary formula in the Israelite oath, well known by the tenth century, and therefore probably much older.[31] To be sure, in poetry and prophecy of a later period we find allusions to the Canaanite myth of creation, the battle with the dragon of chaos, Leviathan or Rahab. One of the clearest of such references is Psalm 74.12-14:

> Yet God is my king of old,
> Working salvation in the midst of the earth.
> Thou didst divide the sea by thy strength;
> Thou brakest the heads of the dragons in the waters.
> Thou brakest the heads of Leviathan in pieces;
> Thou gavest him as food to the people inhabiting the wilderness.

Here the old Canaanite myth of creation has been transferred to Yahweh. The Psalmist is saying that the God who could perform such wonders will surely come to the aid of his people in their distress. Yet this myth is never elaborated in Old Testament literature. In syncretistic circles it may have been taken literally, but in the writings we have it is impossible to tell where reality and metaphor are to be distinguished. In any case, allusions are few before the period of the Exile. On the one hand, the myth was historicized and used metaphorically to describe Yahweh's great victories in history, especially that over Pharaoh's army in the crossing of the Red Sea (e.g. Isa. 51.9-10). On the other hand, it was used in eschatology as a description of God's victory over his enemies in the great Day to come (cf. Isa. 27.1).[32]

[31] In the tenth century document known as the Court History of David it occurs three times: 2 Sam. 12.5, 14.11, 15.21.

[32] For a brief review of the evidence see Howard Wallace, 'Leviathan and the Beast in Revelation,' *Biblical Archaeologist,* Vol. XI (1948), No. 3, pp. 61 ff. Some Scandinavian scholars, who hold that nearly all of the Psalms were originally composed as cultic hymns, believe that from them we can reconstruct an elaborate cult drama of the creation battle similar to that known to have existed in Babylon. They further believe that, as in Babylon, this drama was re-enacted every New Year's Day, with the king playing the role of the God who defeats the dragon of chaos. In so

Israel's religious literature, therefore, was utterly different from that of its environment. Even though the writers borrowed widely from every source, they radically transformed all that was borrowed. The basis of the literature was history, not nature, because the God of Israel was first of all the Lord of history who used nature to accomplish his purposes in history. When modern theologians revive the term 'myth' and use it to describe those portions of the Biblical writing which deal with the supra-historical, with creation and with eschatology, they should make clear that they are using the term in its derived, not primary or original, sense. In the Bible, as distinct from the literature of polytheism, neither the Garden of Eden nor the Kingdom of God are separated from earth or its history; they are firmly fixed in that history. And while they may not fit into the framework of time by which we measure history, they fit into the Biblical sense of historical time, which is nothing else than the time of God's purpose.

These, then, are some of the distinctions which must be drawn between the God of Israel and the gods of the nations. Together they constitute the basis of the Israelite mutation which cannot be comprehended through the metaphor of growth. It is impossible to see how this God of Israel could have evolved slowly from polytheism.[33] The two faiths rest on

doing he renewed the blessing of the original victory for his throne and kingdom during the ensuing year. For an excellent review of the evidence with complete bibliographical citation of the literature, see now Aage Bentzen, *Messias-Moses redivivus-Menschensohn* (Zürich, 1948). While the writer believes that these scholars have thrown considerable light on the theology of the office of king in Israel, he is extremely doubtful about their central thesis concerning the importance in Israel of the yearly re-enactment of a Divine battle-myth. If the thesis were valid, we should have to suppose that Old Testament literature has been radically revised to give central place to the historical event of the Exodus; otherwise we would have more direct references to the cultic drama. Furthermore, it is important that a distinction should be made between literary and cultic forms of literature. The two are not necessarily one and the same thing. (See further Chap. III, Sect. II).

[33] A partial qualification of this statement may possibly be found in

entirely different foundations. The religion of Israel suddenly appears in history, breaking radically with the mythopoeic approach to reality. How are we to explain it, except that it is a new creation? For this reason, there can be no doubt that the fundamental elements of this faith were established *early* in Israel's history, which means that we are led to Sinai and to the work of Moses, like unto whom there did not arise a prophet in Israel (Deut. 34.10). These distinctive elements are the primary data of the Old Testament, that *something* in early Israel which predisposed and predetermined the course of Biblical history.

This is the basic contention of W. F. Albright in his remarkable book, *From the Stone Age to Christianity,* and also in his *Archaeology and the Religion of Israel.* I know of no better summary in abstract terms of the conception of God in early Israel than that which he has given:[34]

> The 'belief in the existence of only one God, who is the Creator of the world and the giver of all life;[35] the belief that God is holy and just, without sexuality or mythology; the belief that God is invisible to man except under special conditions and that no graphic nor plastic representation of Him is permissible; the belief that God is not restricted to any part of His creation, but is equally at home in heaven, in the desert, or in Palestine; the belief that God is so far superior to all created beings, whether heavenly bodies, angelic messengers, demons, or false gods, that He remains absolutely unique; the belief that God has chosen Israel by formal compact to be His favored people, guided exclusively by laws imposed by Him.'

the religion of the Patriarchs and the influence it may have had on Mosaism. The evidence on this point is, however, exceedingly tenuous. For an excellent review of the theology of the earliest histories; those of J and E, see Adam C. Welch, *The Religion of Israel Under the Kingdom* (Edinburgh, 1912), Chap. II.

[34] *Archaeology and the Religion of Israel* (Baltimore, 1942), p. 116.

[35] The time when Israelite leaders began to conceive of God as Creator has been much debated, though in accordance with developmental ideas the conception is generally believed not to be early, and certainly not Mosaic. The earliest witness is, of course, the Yahwist's (J's) material in Genesis 2.4 ff. It is inconceivable that Israel did not possess such a

IV

The quotation from Albright leads us, however, to a consideration of the problem of monotheism. Can this term be used as an adequate description of the religion of early, as well as of late, Israel? Such a complex and vexing question cannot be treated in detail here. For this reason, let us approach the matter from a somewhat different avenue than that ordinarily followed, in order to be sure that we are attacking the problem in its proper context. Let us begin with one of the most difficult passages in the Old Testament, as far as the use of the term monotheism is concerned. That is the 82nd Psalm. A translation is as follows:

(1) God stationed himself in the Divine Assembly (*'adat-El*)
In the midst of the gods (*'elohim*) he has judged:
(2) 'How long will ye give unrighteous judgment,
And respect the persons of the wicked?
(3) 'Judge the poor and fatherless;
The oppressed and impoverished give justice.
(4) 'Rescue the poor and needy
From the hand of the wicked deliver (them).'
(5) They [i.e. the gods] know not; they do not understand;
In darkness they wander about;
All the foundations of the earth are shaken.
(6) I said: 'Gods are ye,
The children of the Most High (*'elyon*), all of ye.

doctrine earlier, both from the standpoint of form criticism and from the fact that creation was a basic concern of all people of the day, at least to judge from polytheistic mythology. Albright bases his contention in part upon the etymology of the name Yahweh. He interprets the word as the causative of the verb 'to be'; as such it means 'he causes to be': that is, he is the Creator (*From the Stone Age to Christianity*, pp. 197 ff.). The writer has been inclined to accept this view on the basis of Albright's arguments, though with an open mind since the case was hardly proved. Now, however, the mounting mass of linguistic evidence from Northwest Semitic is so great that one is forced to admit that no other interpretation can satisfy the linguistic conditions as well as this (see most recently Albright's additional remarks in *Journal of Biblical Literature*, Vol. LXVII, 1948, pp. 379 f.).

(7) 'Yet like man ye shall die,
And like one of the princes ye shall fall.'
(8) Arise, O God;
Judge the earth,
For thou shalt inherit
All the nations.

This Psalm pictures a courtroom scene in which God, as head of the assembly, has indicted some beings called *'elohim* for violating the law (v. 2). He commands them to give justice to the poor and oppressed (vv. 3-4). Then, in an aside (v. 5), he exclaims over the impossibility of their keeping the command. There follows the sentence of death (vv. 6-7). The final verse is the poet's assertion of God's supremacy over all peoples of the earth.

There has been a wide divergence of opinion in the interpretation of this Psalm. The traditional view, of which John 10.34 is the earliest witness, regards the *'elohim* here as human, Israelite judges whom God is sentencing for their failure to provide justice.[36] Such an understanding of the word and of the Psalm is, however, entirely too forced with little to commend it. The same can be said for a suggestion of Duhm that the *'elohim* are the Hasmonean kings and for Buttenwieser's belief that they are the deified kings of the Hellenistic age.[37] We must take more seriously a third view, which as far as I am aware, Ibn Ezra was the first to suggest. In this case the *'elohim* are the patron angels of the nations, who appear in the Book

[36] Cf., for example, John Calvin, *The Book of Psalms,* Vol. 3 (Edinburgh, Calvin Translation Society, 1847), pp. 327 ff.; Franz Delitzsch, *Die Psalmen,* 3rd ed., Zweite Hälfte (Leipzig, 1874), pp. 66 ff.; A. Cohen, *The Psalms* (Hindhead, Surrey, 1945), pp. 270 f.; Davison, *The Psalms,* Vol. II (New York and Edinburgh, n.d.), pp. 93 ff.; A. F. Kirkpatrick, *The Book of Psalms* (Cambridge, 1895), pp. 494 ff.; *The Westminster Study Edition of the Holy Bible* (Philadelphia, 1948), p. 779.

[37] Duhm, *Die Psalmen* (Tübingen, 2nd ed., 1922) pp. 317 f.; M. Buttenwieser, *The Psalms* (Chicago, 1938), pp. 769 f.; Cf. Frdr. Baethgen, *Die Psalmen* (Göttingen, 1897), pp. 252 ff.

of Daniel and extra-canonical literature.[38]. Yet it is a question as to whether the patron angels of late theology would have been condemned to death as are the *'elohim* of this Psalm.[39]

In any event this third view differs but slightly from a fourth interpretation, espoused by such scholars as Gunkel and Wellhausen. In this case the Psalm is taken literally. God calls the gods of the nations to a heavenly assize, named here *'adat-El*. He, as the head of the assembly and its judge, indicts them for their failure to provide justice for the poor and needy. So great are their misdeeds, committed in the darkness of their understanding, that the foundations of the universal order are shaken. Consequently, the sentence of death like that of a mortal, is placed upon them.[40]

There is a large amount of evidence in the Old Testament

[38] Cf. A. C. Welch, *The Psalter* (Oxford, 1926), pp. 41 f.; and the discussion in Baethgen, *loc. cit.,* and Cohen, *loc. cit.*

[39] Dr. Bernard J. Bamberger kindly informs me that in those works of Jewish literature 'that mention fallen angels, we read of their imprisonment and punishment, but not as a rule of their death. There are, however, a few exceptions: Talmud *Babli Makkot* 12a, and Eisenstein, *Ozar Midrashim,* pp. 191-2, 193b. Both these passages are exceptional, and the second comes from an obscure source without claim to authority.' By all odds the best and most instructive treatment of Ps. 82 of which I am aware is that of Julian Morgenstern, *Hebrew Union College Annual,* Vol. XIV (Cincinnati, 1939), pp. 29-126. Yet with his central thesis I find it impossible to agree. He believes that of the original Psalm remaining in the present edition are vv. 1, 5c, 6-7. The remainder, particularly vv. 2-4 concerning the indictment, he believes to have been composed as a substitute for the original lines when the latter appeared too offensive. The clue to the original indictment he finds in Gen. 6.1-4, and interprets it as concerning the fallen angels. There is no doubt that his reconstruction makes excellent sense, but in reality it is tearing a short composition to pieces on tenuous evidence in order to rebuild it according to one's own notions.

[40] Cf. H. Gunkel, *Ausgewählte Psalmen* (Göttingen, 1904), pp. 129 ff.; J. Wellhausen, *The Book of Psalms; A New English Translation* (New York, 1898), p. 198; Hans Schmidt, *Die Psalmen* (Tübingen, 1934), pp. 156 f.; W. O. E. Oesterley, *The Psalms* (London, 1939), Vol. II, pp. 373 ff.; and most recently Elmer Leslie, *The Psalms* (New York and Nashville, 1949), pp. 120 ff.

for the heavenly assembly or council, presided over by God and composed of Divine attendants, heralds, and administrators.[41] Various words were used for them: *mal'akim* ('angels,' properly 'messengers'), *qedoshim* ('holy ones'), *bene 'elohim* or *bene 'elim* ('sons of god' or divine beings), *'abadim* (servants), *mesharetim* ('ministers'). The first three of these terms appear also in Ugaritic.[42] All members of the council are occasionally designated *saba* ('host'), particularly in the phrase 'host of heaven.' I need only refer here to the vision of the prophet Micaiah in 1 Kings 22.19: 'I saw Yahweh sitting upon his throne, and all the host of heaven (*seba hash-shamayim*) standing by him on his right hand and on his left.'[43] For the Divine assembly itself the familiar Hebrew words for human assemblies and councils are used: in addition to the *'eda* of Psalm 82, are also *mo'ed, sod* and *qahal.* Of these terms only *mo'ed* and *'eda* appear in similar context in Ugaritic; there the word *pukhru*, as also in Accadian, is the more customary name for the council.[44]

That this conception of a Divine Assembly appears in the earliest, as well as in the latest, literature of the Old Testament is evident not only from the JE strata of the Pentateuch,[45] but also from the early poem in Deut. 33 (The Blessing of Moses).[46] In addition we note Ex. 15 (the Song of Miriam, v. 11 LXX),

[41] For an interesting, though brief, article on the subject, see H. Wheeler Robinson, 'The Council of Yahweh,' *Journal of Theological Studies*, Vol. 45 (1944), pp. 151 ff.

[42] See C. H. Gordon, *Ugaritic Handbook*, Vol. III, words 119, 395, 1060 (though only human messengers are listed, the word will certainly be found of divine sooner or later), 1768.

[43] Cf. also Job. 1-2, and Morgenstern, *op. cit.*, pp. 40 ff.

[44] Gordon, *loc. cit.*, words 1202 and 1455.

[45] The frequent mention of angels in the Pentateuch presupposes the assembly. Cf. also Gen. 3.22 ('Behold man is become like *one from us*'; the sin of man is that he has exerted himself to possess a knowledge like that possessed by a member of the heavenly council).

[46] For the latest treatment of this poem, see Frank M. Cross, Jr., and David Noel Freedman, 'The Blessing of Moses,' *Journal of Biblical Literature*, Vol. LXVII (1948), pp. 191 ff.

Psalms 29 and 89, should the date of these also be accepted as belonging to the period of the early monarchy.[47]

A wealth of comparative material for the conception is available in both Accadian and Canaanite literature, though there is opportunity here only to mention the well-known fact that it exists.[48] It is in this context, it seems to me, that the age-old exclamation of praise, evidently borrowed by Israel from her neighbors, 'Who is like unto thee among the Gods, O Yahweh,' is primarily to be interpreted. Is it probable that an Israelite would have meant this exclamation any more henotheistically than would a Babylonian or Canaanite: namely, that in the whole assembly of heaven, none is comparable to the head of the assembly?[49]

In the light of the evidence the literal interpretation of Psalm 82 must, it seems to me, be accepted as the only possible one. The problem which immediately arises, however, is in regard to the composition of the heavenly council. There appears to be considerable evidence that during the seventh and sixth

[47] These are poems which possess many allusions to Canaanite literature, and the tendency now is to date them early. Psalm 29 has been shown to have been borrowed directly from Canaan: cf. H. L. Ginsberg, *Biblical Archaeologist,* Vol. VIII (1945), No. 2, pp. 53 f.; and T. H. Gaster, *Jewish Quarterly Review*, Vol. 37 (1946-47), pp. 55 ff.

[48] See especially the treatment by T. Jacobsen of the Mesopotamian evidence, in *The Intellectual Adventure of Ancient Man,* Chaps. V and VI.

[49] See the writer's remarks in *Biblical Archaeologist,* Vol. VI (1943), No. 1, p. 14. Cf. especially Ps. 89.6-8 and 95.3 where the comparison to the heavenly host is explicitly made. In most cases, however, it is doubtful whether this frequent type of comparative expression involves anything more than an honorific ascription to God (e.g. 2 Sam. 7.22; 1 Kings 8.23; Ps. 35.10, 71.19, 77.13, etc.). The ascription is simply borrowed from a pagan context and used of Yahweh, any *definite* comparative notion having fallen into the background. An exception to the general statement might be Jer. 10.6 (cf. also Ps. 96.4), where the comparative is used in a context which expresses the worthlessness of other gods. In this case the gods of the nations are definitely meant and nothing is said about the assembly conception. The gods are merely idols (see further below).

centuries, at least, a large amount of syncretism occurred, so that within the framework of the council a number of pagan elements appear. In any event, we know that in this period and later the host of heaven, meaning the sun, moon, and stars, appear as members of the assembly. The post-exilic public confession of sin in Neh. 9.6 speaks of Yahweh's making the heavens and all their host; and it is said, 'the host of heaven worshippeth thee.' Psalm 148 begins:

> Praise ye Yahweh from the heavens,
> Praise him in the heights;
> Praise ye him, all his angels;
> Praise ye him, all his hosts;
> Praise ye him, sun and moon;
> Praise him, all ye stars of light.

The Deuteronomists and Jeremiah exhibit a sharp reaction against the paganizing of Yahwism made possible by the inclusion of the heavenly bodies in the assembly. Manasseh erected altars to them in the very courts of the temple (2 Kings 21.3-5). Jeremiah speaks of people burning incense on housetops to all the host of heaven and pouring out drink offerings to other gods (Chap. 19.13). Nevertheless the stars continued as members of the assembly in the Post-Exilic period, though it was not permitted to give them independent worship.

Psalm 82 goes a step farther, however, with its actual inclusion in the assembly of the gods of the nations, who have been given by God responsibility for the welfare of the peoples of the world. This recalls the early reference in Deut. 33.3 to the holy ones who are 'the guardians of the peoples,' to use the rendering of Cross and Freedman;[50] and also the reference in Deut. 32.8-9 where the correct text, preserved by the Septuagint, speaks of God's apportioning the nations and establishing 'the boundaries of the peoples according to the number of the divine beings (*bene 'elim*),' though he himself has kept Israel as his special possession. I find it difficult to regard these references

[50] *Loc. cit.*, pp. 193 and 200.

as mere metaphors or as accommodating modes of speech. The actual existence of the other gods is here assumed. The point is that they are without independent existence; they are responsible to the head of the council, Yahweh, who in Psalm 82 actually sentences them to a most ungodlike fate, death, after the manner of a mortal.

To understand the Israelite manner of thought, I think it is important to note that Israel did not conceive of an inanimate nature any more than did polytheists. While breaking radically with polytheism, the Israelite like the early Greek philosopher[51] continued to think of the elements of nature as possessing a psychic life of their own. When the prophet proclaims God's indictment of Israel with the words, 'Hear, O heavens and give ear, O earth,' (Isa. 1.2), or 'Hear, O ye mountains, Yahweh's controversy, and ye enduring rocks, the foundations of the earth,' (Micah 6.2), is he speaking in pure metaphor, or only partially so? Must we not interpret such passages in the light of the Divine Assembly, the members of which constitute the host of heaven and of earth?

In the past the chief problem in the paganizing of Yahwism has been conceived as lying in the identification in some measure of Yahweh with Baal. I would suggest that the far greater danger lay in the conception of the Divine assembly which resembles so closely the assemblies of polytheism. What is the precise difference between an assembly of divine beings presided over by Yahweh and that headed by Baal or Marduk? The ambiguity here is plain, and it is one which Israel did not entirely escape. That there was a great difference is clear on a moment's reflection, but can that difference be comprehended by either of the rather artificial terms of modern scholarship, 'henotheism' or 'monotheism'? Henotheism in Old Testament scholarship has been conceived as the worship of one God who is confined to one's own people and country, but a worship

[51] Cf. H. and H. A. Frankfort in *Intellectual Adventure of Ancient Man*, pp. 373 ff.

which does not exclude the recognition of other deities. Such a definition certainly does not fit the universal and cosmic conception implicit in the Divine assembly. Nor is it possible to portray a development in the Old Testament comprehension of the assembly from henotheism to monotheism. In fact, if one were forced to argue the question, he might maintain that the development is in the opposite direction, since the assembly undeniably became more complex during the course of time. It is probable that Psalm 82 belongs to a period between the seventh and fourth centuries B.C., though it must be admitted that we have no certain means of dating it. If it is late, then it belongs to the age which scholars have heretofore agreed was definitely monotheistic. If the terms 'monotheism' and 'henotheism' are to be used, then either the whole of the Old Testament, including Second Isaiah[52] and the Chronicles, is henotheistic, or else it is monotheistic. Following the lead of W. F. Albright,[53] I still prefer the word 'monotheism,' because it has always been used to define Judaism and Christianity in which the angelic host has survived and has even been elaborated. Yet for the Old Testament itself, the word can only be used, as in the case of Psalm 82, with a clear understanding of what one means and of the distinctions which must necessarily be made.

Furthermore, the very difference between the Israelite and pagan Divine assemblies argues in favor of the term monotheism over against henotheism. In Israel there was an exclusive and true monolatry,[54] which did not exist elsewhere. The

[52] As Frank M. Cross, Jr., has pointed out to me, Isa. 40 must probably be interpreted as beginning with a scene in the heavenly assembly, where God instructs his angels to comfort Jerusalem (the verb translated 'comfort ye' is active and must not be interpreted as 'Be ye comforted'). Cf. Isa. 40.26 also.

[53] See *From the Stone Age to Christianity,* pp. 196 ff., and *Journal of Biblical Literature,* Vol. LIX (1940), pp. 85 ff.

[54] The term 'monolatry' is one which some scholars would prefer to use to the exclusion of 'henotheism' or 'monotheism.' Yet its real

members of the assembly were to receive no independent worship. Psalm 82 even envisages the death of the gods and the assumption of direct, rather than delegated, control over the nations by the head of the assembly himself (v. 8). The God of Israel so transcends all things in heaven and earth that he is conceived as their sole creator. The members of his assembly, the belief in which is a survival or borrowing from polytheism possess no independent authority or even existence or worship. Their being and authority are derived, not primary. The believer is led by them to the worship of their source, Yahweh; *they* are thoroughly devaluated while *he* is exalted. So intense was this exclusive exaltation that the doctrine of God's jealousy, so utterly different from the tolerance and easy balance of opposing forces characteristic of the very nature of polytheism, became central in Israelite theology. This doctrine, so offensive to the naturalist and mystic of every age, is precisely the one which raised the problem for Israel of the relation between the revealed religion and the mythopoeic naturalisms of the surrounding peoples. The problem of 'other gods' was thus acute for Israel in a way not comprehensible to the naturalistic polytheist.

Furthermore, the very exaltation of God's power in Israel meant the complete devaluation of all other powers. Johannes Hehn pointed out years ago in his *Die biblische und die*

significance has rarely been examined. A true monolatry such as existed in Israel was a phenomenal thing in that ancient world; when coupled with those other conceptions described here and in Section III of this chapter, it differed radically even from the ephemeral and artificial monotheism of Ikhnaton of Egypt (in which the king remained as the incarnation of the sun-god and in which there was little sense of history or of social justice according to Biblical standards). The limitation of the term 'monolatry' is that properly it describes only liturgical practice. Mr. Edmund Perry of Garrett Biblical Institute has suggested the term 'monarchotheism' for the religion of Israel. This suggestion has the advantage of preserving the central metaphor of Israel's faith; though like all metaphors it too has its limitations. Furthermore, it would appear that any monotheism must be monarchic.

babylonische Gottesidee,[55] a remarkable book for its time though for some reason largely neglected, that Israelite monotheism was not derived from philosophical speculation concerning the one and the many, but from a knowledge of God's power, expressed in powerful acts. It was by the power of this one God that a people without the law were given a law, that the several tribes and extraneous clans became one nation. When in later Israel, the gods of the nations are derided as 'no-gods,' there is no abstract or metaphysical emphasis on the existence or non-existence of these gods, but instead the emphasis is on their lack of power to do anything. And a god without power was unworthy of any consideration other than derision![56]

To my mind the term 'henotheism' does not do justice to these facts. But when we use the term 'monotheism' for Israelite faith, we must make clear that we are not using the term in a Greek speculative sense. The word 'henotheism' does avoid the ambiguity involved in the attempt to force a philosophical monism upon Israelite religious faith. But the value of the word 'monotheism' lies in its emphasis upon *the most characteristic and unique feature of Israel: the exclusive exaltation of the one source of all power, authority, and creativity.*

What, after all, is Psalm 82 saying? Implicit here is a typically Israelite explanation of the existence of phenomena. It is a fact that other peoples have other gods. Why? Because God has so determined it. But the other gods have not fulfilled their

[55] Leipzig, 1913, p. 277.

[56] It is probable that the problem of other gods is not dealt with uniformly in the Old Testament in the light of the Divine assembly. The prophetic devaluation of the other gods is perhaps still another approach to the problem. As far as monotheism is concerned, however, the result of the two approaches is approximately the same. Furthermore, it should perhaps be stated that in the history of human thought and experience there are many different forms of monotheism: cf. Millar Burrows, *Jewish Quarterly Review*, Vol. 33 (1942-43), pp. 476 ff., and Josiah Royce, 'Monotheism,' in Hastings' *Encyclopaedia of Religion and Ethics* (Edinburgh, 1916).

commission, and the foundations of earth are shaken. So God has withdrawn his commission and condemned the gods to death. For it is he, and he alone, who can and will provide a just and lasting universal order.

If we are denied the use of the term 'monotheism' for such an existential point of view, then we shall experience considerable difficulty in finding the precise point at which it can be introduced into the Judeo-Christian scene. There is not only the problem of the developed angelogy and demonology of later Judaism; there is also the question of defining the Godhead of the New Testament. There the various orders of the supernatural are much more complex than in the Old Testament. God the Father, the Creator of all things and the ultimate authority in the universe, has exalted Christ to his right hand, and has put all things in subjection to him. Both the Apostle Paul and the evangelist John speak of Christ as the first-born of creation or as the pre-existent Word of God, by whom all things in heaven and earth were created (John 1 and Col. 1.15 ff.). The angels, archangels and the whole host of heaven are in subjection to him (cf. Heb. 1-2, 1 Peter 3.22, etc.). Yet these heavenly powers, subservient to God and to his Christ, must not receive independent worship. To accord them such would spoil the 'simplicity that is in Christ' (2 Cor. 11.3; cf. especially Col. 2.18 and Heb. 1.6 ff.). There is yet another realm, however, one composed of principalities and powers, the 'spiritual hosts of wickedness' against which we wrestle (e.g. Eph. 6.12), though our victory is assured through Christ.

Superficially, this New Testament portrayal of God the Father and of Christ the exalted Lord and King reminds one of the polytheistic juxtaposition of passive authority in the head of the pantheon and of executive authority in the divine king of the gods and men. Yet the resemblance obviously is only a formal one and ceases at that point. To continue the discussion would lead us to the Christological controversies of the early Church which resulted in the affirmation of the unity of God under the formula of the Trinity. Obviously, no dictionary ever intended to exclude early Christianity from the definition of monotheism in favor of a purely abstract unitarianism.[57]

We must not forget, however, that this discussion of monotheism is largely an academic affair, pursued because we feel the need to define Biblical faith according to Hellenic rather than Hebrew categories of thought. While in the present world we must of necessity make rational distinctions, we should not be led by them into a betrayal of the data with which we are dealing. Biblical religion is centered in an anthropomorphic vocabulary, in God the 'Lord' who 'chose' Israel for himself and in God the 'Father' of our 'Lord' Jesus Christ. It is not centered in the Absolute of metaphysical speculation any more than it is centered in the cycle of nature.

[57] Professor Sherman E. Johnson has pointed out to me that 1 Cor. 8.4-6 and 10.19-21 indicate that in the New Testament strict philosophical monotheism was no more prevalent than in the Old. In these passages the existence of other beings is not altogether denied, but they are degraded to the rank of demons (cf. also Clement of Alexandria, *Exhortation to the Heathen*). For an interesting treatment of monotheism in relation to trinitarian theology, see Professor Johnson's article, 'Thoughts on Early Christian Monotheism,' *Anglican Theological Review*, Vol. XXXI, No. 2 (April, 1949), pp. 103-111.

CHAPTER TWO

'HE ESTABLISHED A TESTIMONY IN ISRAEL'

I

IN THE first chapter an attempt was made to describe some of those primary elements in the Israelite knowledge of God which could not have been derived from a polytheistic environment. Yet we have accomplished nothing more than a definition of the basis upon which the Israelite phenomenon of monotheism was established. It would be quite wrong to assume that this type of enquiry focuses attention upon the central concerns of Old Testament faith. Is it simply an accident that Israelite writers did not provide us with at least a few well-chosen sentences to tell us what they actually believed about the real existence of other gods? To us it is strangely disconcerting that they were so unconcerned with this matter. Of course, they lived in an age which was largely innocent of that type of logical reasoning which the world has learned from the Greeks. They expressed what they knew more by means of picture, story, and metaphor than they did by the language of abstraction. Is this, however, all that is to be said? Is it possible that our concern with the definition of monotheism is largely an academic affair, at least from the standpoint of Biblical faith?

The study of comparative religion can do nothing more than point out the distinctiveness, and perhaps the superiority, of the Biblical God; it cannot lead us into the presence of this God, nor can it bring us to worship him or to acknowledge him as *our* God. For this reason the Israelite man of faith could not have been more than mildly interested in our Chapter I! More to his liking would have been a discussion of Elijah's challenge on Mount Carmel: 'How long are ye to limp upon a divided opinion? If Yahweh is God, go after him; if Baal, go after him!' (1 Kings 18.21). Biblical faith is a challenge to commitment, and even the historical literature as we have it was edited, preserved, and for the most part originally written with this definite evangelical purpose. The issue is not the careful weighing of the various merits of the gods. It is rather: 'Who is God? Decide on the evidence and act accordingly!' What is the evidence? It is the evidence of history. What God has the power to do what he wills and to fulfil what he promises? Virtually the only comparative religion which the Old Testament possesses is of this type. Baal could do nothing, with the result that Elijah could ironically say: 'Perhaps he is musing, or on a journey, or asleep!'

The worship of other gods in the Old Testament meant weakness, trouble and defeat for the worshippers. This is nowhere better expressed than in the Song of Moses (Deut. 32).[1] There it is said that Yahweh alone has been the leader of Israel; no foreign god was with him in the great triumphs of the past. But Israel is a people void of counsel and understanding who follow a 'No-God.' When their power is completely dissipated, through idolatry, when one says: 'Where are their gods, the rock in which they trusted? Let them rise up and help you, let them be your protection'—then Yahweh will say:

> 'See now that I
> Even I am he,
> And there is no God with me!
> I kill and make alive;
> I wound and I heal
> And there is no deliverer from my hand!'

The power of Yahweh, who alone reigns for ever and ever and beside whom everything in heaven and earth is impotent—such is the dominant characteristic of the God of Israel which the writers love to emphasize in the most forceful terms. This power is a positive thing, one that is intolerant of presumption,

[1] It is impossible to date this poem with any certainty, except to assert that in its present form it probably belongs to the period between the ninth and sixth centuries B.C.

pride or high-handedness on the part of any man or group of men who dare to set themselves and their idols athwart the Divine will. The doctrine of God's jealousy produced in Israel such a sharpening of issues as to keep the worshipper in a state of tension, never completely integrated with the state of affairs that existed within him or without.

At this point we encounter a distinct contrast between the faith of Israel and that of the polytheist. The latter lives in a world that is more tolerant, one in which the emphasis is upon order, harmony and integration. The worlds of society, nature and the gods interpenetrate in such a way that the *status quo* is the focus of attention. The aim of the gods is to preserve the established order, and the whole cultic and social life of man is primarily aimed at integration with the sacrosanct economy of the world. In the Egyptian wisdom literature, for example, the contrast repeatedly made is between the 'passionate man' and the 'silent man.' The latter is the successful man because he is always calm and never a disturber of the established order. The former, on the other hand, is the bad man because his passionate self-assertiveness 'destroys that harmonious integration in the existing order which alone is effective.'[2] It is small

[2] Frankfort, *Ancient Egyptian Religion*, (New York, 1948) pp. 65 ff. Contrast the wisdom of Israel, the pagan source of which, as exemplified by the Book of Proverbs, is well known. One writer has gone so far as to speak of the early seekers after wisdom in Israel as natural men, unaided by special revelation (Rylaarsdam, *Revelation in Jewish Wisdom Literature,* Chicago, 1946, p. 72). It is true that Proverbs lacks the prophetic emphasis on election, history and eschatology. It is a special category of literature with its own individual style and form, largely determined in the pagan environment before being taken over by Israel. What is not sufficiently emphasized, however, is the difference between the Hebrew Proverbs and those of the contemporary paganism. This difference is not always to be seen in the comparison of individual sayings; it exists primarily in conceptual background. In Israel the contrast is no longer between the 'silent' and the 'passionate' man, but between the 'righteous' and the 'wicked,' presupposing an entirely different theological platform on which wisdom is erected. The knowledge of righteousness and wickedness presupposes a revealed law. The reiter-

wonder, therefore, that all polytheisms tend to be religions of the *status quo* and that none of them has ever produced a thoroughgoing social revolution based upon a high concept of social justice. Revolution of any sort is abhorrent to the inmost nature of such natural religion.

In the Bible, however, a state of tension exists between God and creation. To be sure, God created the social order by the revelation of his will and law. But the *revealed* order and the *actual* order are never identical except in the eschatological age to which history is moving by the direction and intervention of God. A profound disharmony exists between the will of God and the existing social order. God in his redemptive work stands in judgment upon man for his sin, and the startling affirmation is made that man and his society can only be redeemed through the purifying fire of Divine judgment. The Israelite desired peace and harmony as deeply as any man, but he lived for the most part in a world of disharmony. Consequently, revolution was expected; even though feared, it was seen to be a necessity before the revealed order could be consummated. It has been well said that

> 'in Egypt and Mesopotamia man was dominated, but also supported, by the great rhythm of nature. If in his dark moments he felt himself caught and held in the net of unfathomable decisions, his involvement in nature had, on the whole, a soothing character. He was gently carried along on the perennial cosmic tides of the seasons. The depth and intimacy of man's relationship with nature found

ated emphasis on obeying and fearing Yahweh who is the source of wisdom (with which he created the world in 3.19, 8.22 ff.) leads to the same conclusion. For this reason, the following statement of H. Wheeler Robinson commends itself (*Inspiration and Revelation in the Old Testament,* Oxford, 1946, p. 241): 'Prophecy alone explains the characteristic qualities and the theocratic emphasis of Israel's Wisdom over against the qualities of the international wisdom (not itself without relation to various types of religion of a very different kind from that of Israel). We may, in fact, define the Wisdom of Israel as the discipline *whereby was taught the application of prophetic truth to the individual life in the light of experience.*'

expression in the ancient symbol of the mother-goddess. But Hebrew thought ignored this image entirely. . . . The doctrine of a single, unconditioned, transcendent God rejected time-honoured values, proclaimed new ones, postulated a metaphysical significance for history and man's actions. With infinite *moral* courage the Hebrews worshipped an absolute God and accepted as the correlate of their faith the sacrifice of a harmonious existence.'[3]

It is not surprising, therefore, that the most energetic movements for social reform have occurred in those countries heavily influenced by this Judeo-Christian point of view. Indeed, in Israel itself they occurred repeatedly. In the words of Professor Albright: 'Protected by religious sanctions, the prophets of Judah were a reforming political force which has never been surpassed and perhaps never equalled in subsequent world-history.' As direct spokesmen or heralds of the Divine Lord, they created an extraordinary atmosphere of social and political reform entirely unknown in polytheistic circles; their 'freedom of speech put Hyde Park and the best days of muckraking newspapers to shame.'[4]

II

Accompanying this sense of tension between the revealed and the actual orders of society was a peculiar tendency toward exclusivism or particularism in the operation of the Divine love. God had many people, but he reserved a special love for one people. Of all the families of the earth he chose one for special blessing (cf. Gen. 12.1-3). Here is a different kind of love from that of the wide-hearted love of the world comprehended in the Greek *Eros*.[5] It is a particular love which expresses itself in election.

[3] *Intellectual Adventure of Ancient Man*, pp. 371, 373.

[4] *Approaches to World Peace* (New York, Council on Science, Philosophy and Religion, 1943), pp. 9 f.

[5] So E. Stauffer in G. Kittel, ed. *Theologisches Wörterbuch zum Neuen Testament*, Vol. 1 (Stuttgart, 1933), pp. 38 f.

The Old Testament doctrine of a chosen people, one selected by God 'for his own possession above all the people that are on the face of the earth' (Deut. 7.6), is the chief clue for the understanding of the meaning and significance of Israel. Here is the focal point of the literature, one of the central factors which distinguish it from all other religious literatures. The peculiarly Israelite point of view toward the apprehension of the Divine is to be seen, not primarily in abstract discussion of the merits of the one over against the many, but in the fact that the God of the Bible is first of all and pre-eminently the 'God of Israel.'

The ancient objection of Celsus against this Biblical claim of a unique revelation to a chosen people still expresses one of the main difficulties which people have with the Old Testament. According to Celsus, the Jew and the Christian claim that God made the whole world and the vault of heaven for them in particular: 'God, having abandoned the heavenly regions, and despising this great earth, takes up His abode among us alone, and to us alone makes His announcements, and ceases not His messages and enquiries as to how we may become His associates forever.'[6] A God of love and justice, it is claimed, could scarcely exhibit such favoritism. Our tendency toward strong objection to this central claim of Israel for herself has evidently made it difficult for old Testament scholarship to give the doctrine the attention it deserves. We find it much simpler to assume that the claim was simply the expression of a people's feeling of superiority, or better their over-compensation for an inferiority complex.

The answers to these objections are obvious. What a terrible price was paid by Israel for this election! The story Israel tells of herself is a sordid, sorry tale. What glory there is in it is accredited solely to the love and grace of God, who wrought so wonderfully for his people in the early days, but who because

[6] Origen, *Contra Celsum* (*Ante-Nicene Christian Library*, Vol. XXIII, Edinburgh, 1872), Book IV, Chaps. 27-28.

of his people's sin humbled their natural and national aspirations by the fires of tribulation. The election of Israel was not one of special privilege alone, and the story of Israel as told by her own writers is utterly different from that of overweening nationalisms. There is something fixed and unchangeable about the God of Israel; he is an external point of reference. He was no mere personification of group prejudice and ambition; he is portrayed as in continual conflict with the people's desires. With a dynamic, persistent and independent energy, he set his course and that of his people for his own name's sake. The familiar words of Amos indicate the terrible burden that election carried: 'You only have I known of all the families of the earth. Therefore, I shall visit upon you all your iniquities' (Am. 3.2). As Wm. Robertson Smith once put it, 'if Israel would not learn to know Jehovah in the good land of Canaan, it must once more pass through the desert and enter the door of hope through the valley of tribulation.'[7] The contemporary natural and cultural religions declined and perished when the civilizations were destroyed which they buttressed. But not so in Israel! A majority of the nation was described as given over to superstition while the political leaders manipulated their skeptical politics. Yet Yahweh 'was never without a remnant that read the facts of history in another light, and saw in them the proof, not that Jehovah was powerless or indifferent, but that He was engaged in a great controversy with His people, a controversy that had moral issues unseen by those who knew not Jehovah and neglected the only service in which He was well pleased.'[8]

The simple honesty of the Israelite writers in describing both the election and the sin of people and national heroes is a phenomenal fact, more unique even in the ancient world than it is in the modern. Before the great eternal Lord the writers had honesty forced upon them. In that presence a remarkably

[7] *The Prophets of Israel* (London, 2nd ed. 1895), pp. 69-70.
[8] *Ibid.*

candid and profound understanding of the true nature of a human being, both his good and his evil, was attained.

Furthermore, we must ask what Israel meant by her claim of special election. By comparison of herself with others did she arrive at the conclusion that of course she was superior and therefore chosen? In the literature of the Old Testament it is quite possible to find a generous dash of that type of reasoning, but it was stronger in the later periods of the history than in the earlier. Israel's chief claim for herself could scarcely have arisen in this fashion. The tendency toward self-righteousness which arose from a comparison with others did not originate but merely buttressed a conception already present.

The real explanation is a simple one. The doctrine of the Chosen People arose as the natural explanation of a historical fact. Israel as an oppressed minority group in Egypt was marvelously delivered, led through a bleak, inhospitable wilderness, and given a land in which to dwell. That was a simple fact. The Israelite reasoned from fact and event in the light of his knowledge of God. Moses was a remarkable leader, but it was Yahweh who had chosen him and overcome his hesitancy. To the Israelite it was nothing short of miraculous that a great Divine Lord should so take pity on this people, should be so interested in an oppressed minority group, that he should engage in a fateful struggle with Pharaoh, the greatest temporal power of the day, and emerge the victor for their cause. These events were the conclusive proof, not only of God's power and might, but also of his gracious concern for Israel. The Psalmists sang in awe, in praise, and in thanksgiving at the great deliverance. Prophets appealed to the conscience of the people and warned of the results of ingratitude and unfaithfulness. Who was Yahweh? Nearly all of Israel's theological confessions were based on the formula repeated in varying forms: 'He is the God who brought us out of the land of Egypt, out of the house of bondage.'

The Exodus or deliverance from Egypt, therefore, is the

central or focal point in Israelite history and faith. When Israel claimed to be the Chosen People, she was giving the only explanation possible to her for this historical event. Looking back at the tradition of the Fathers it was only natural that the doctrine of election should be traced to Abram, the Patriarchal father of the people (Gen. 12.1-3), as the sole explanation for his leaving home and kindred for a land of which he knew nothing.[9] In all of our main historical sources the deliverance from Egypt is seen as the fulfilment of God's promises to the Patriarchs. This is especially clear in the J stratum of Genesis and Exodus, in which the framework is precisely that of promise and fulfilment. Yahweh calls Abraham and makes the election promise to him. That promise is repeated to each of the Patriarchs.[10] The Exodus and the conquest then follow as a witness to Yahweh's faithfulness to his promises.[11] The Priestly editors and the Book of Deuteronomy possess the same point of view.

Why did God choose Israel? If Israel's claim for herself had arisen late in her history as a result of a comparison with others, then we should expect a clear and consistent answer to this question. As it is, the later writers take the matter for granted and look upon it as the supreme manifestation of Divine grace. The Deuteronomist explains: 'Yahweh did not set his love on you, nor choose you because ye were more in number than any people—for ye were the fewest of all peoples—but because Yahweh loved you and because he would keep the oath which he swore unto your fathers' (Deut. 7.7-8). The same author further warns Israel not to become self-righteous about the matter. After the successful conclusion of the conquest, the

[9] For an analysis of the double tradition of election, one dating from the time of Abraham and the other from the time of Moses, see especially K. Galling, *Die Erwählungstraditionen Israels (Beihefte zur Zeitschrift für die Alttestamentliche Wissenschaft,* 48), Giessen, 1928. Cf. also, H. Wheeler Robinson, *op. cit.,* chap. XI.

[10] To Abraham, Gen. 12.1-3; to Isaac, 26.24; to Jacob, 28.13-15.

[11] For specific J phrasing see, e.g., Ex. 13.11, 33.1-3; Num. 10.29; Deut. 34.4.

people are not to think that God had thrust out the nations because Israel was the more righteous, 'whereas for the wickedness of these nations Yahweh doth drive them out from before thee. Not for thy righteousness, or for the uprightness of thy heart, dost thou go in to possess their land; but for the wickedness of these nations . . . and that he may establish the word which Yahweh swore unto thy fathers, to Abraham, to Isaac, and to Jacob' (Deut. 9.4-5).

Yet why did God swear an oath with the Fathers? That is, why did he choose Abraham? The only answer preserved in the early literature is that given five different times in the JE (Yahwish and Elohist) strata of Genesis. The simple formula of J has been translated as follows: 'In thee shall all the families of the earth *be blessed*' (Gen. 12.3; 28.14; cf. 18.18). Two E passages (Gen. 22.18, 26.4) which express the same thought in slightly different wording—'In thy seed shall all the families of the earth *bless themselves*' (Hebrew)—prove that the verb 'to bless' as used in all of these passages must be understood in a reflexive sense.[12] The thought is that God has chosen Israel in order that all people of the earth may use her name in the formula by which they seek blessing for themselves. Through the ancient conception of blessing the writers are saying that God's purpose is to use Israel for a universal blessing.[13] The

[12] The J passages use the niphal conjugation of the root *barak*, while E employs the hithpael. As we should expect, Jeremiah 4.2 is dependent upon the latter tradition ('In him shall the nations bless themselves').

[13] We must beware of attempts which reduce the meaning of these JE statements to a primitive and crude magic; that is, to interpret them as meaning nothing more than that other nations by the magical form of a blessing will appropriate to themselves the blessings of Israel. Such thought is completely foreign to the high theological tone of JE and to the clear purpose of the writers. They possess a view of history in which a plan of God exists and in which Abraham and his seed are to play a crucial role. The blessings of mankind are viewed as dependent on the faith of Abraham. Cf. Driver, *The Book of Genesis* (New York and London, 1904), p. 145, and *Sermons on the Old Testament* (London, 1892), pp. 50 ff.; L. E. P. Erith in *A New Commentary on the Holy Scripture*, edited by Gore *et al.* (New York, 1928), p. 49; Carpenter and

two different traditions as to the wording of the formula indicate that this thought is probably far older than either J or E and rests on very early tradition. The Deuteronomic and Priestly writers do not develop the universalism of this early explanation of the meaning of God's election. Prophetic eschatology (e.g. Isa. 2.2-4; Micah 4.1-4), Second Isaiah and the Book of Jonah, however, do elaborate its meaning, in different directions, while it finds further expression in the later Jewish proselyte movement and especially in the New Testament doctrine of the atonement.

This interpretation of the meaning of these passages in Genesis is further buttressed by the setting of election in the total plan of history as conceived by the J document. In the description of the prehistoric age (Gen. 2-11) the primary concern of this document is with the plight of man in this life. Driven from Paradise because of his rebellion against his Creator, man faces a life of continual struggle against temptation on the one hand, and a recalcitrant nature on the other (Gen. 3.15-19). Civilization advances by successive stages, and man's progress in the civilized arts corresponds with the growth of his sin. The first clothes (Gen. 3.7, 21) and the cultivation of the soil are associated with the fall of man from his primeval state of innocence. In the present edition of the narrative Cain the agrarian murderer is associated with Cain the builder of the first city (Gen. 4.17). Progress in the arts of nomadism, metallurgy and music culminate in the completely hardened and

Harford, *The Composition of the Hexateuch* (London, 1902), pp. 175 ff., 200 ff. It is agreed by all scholars that these verses do not necessarily mean that the *faith* of Israel is to become the faith of all mankind (cf. Gunkel, *Genesis,* Göttingen, 1901, pp. 151 ff.). The point on which there is disagreement is whether the election of Abraham possesses a redemptive significance for the world. In the light of the plan of history as presented, especially in J, I feel it is necessary to side with those who answer this question in the affirmative. Thus the versions, Ecclesiasticus 44.21, Acts 3.25, and Gal. 3.8, while mistakenly translating the verbs in the passive, were not without justification. See now especially G. von Rad, *Das erste Buch Mose, Genesis, Kapitel 1-12,9* (Göttingen, 1949), 15 f., 132 ff.

vengeful Lamech (Gen. 4.18-24). With the planting of vineyards we are presented with a picture of a good man drunk (Gen. 9.20 ff.). The growth and separation of nations and languages is associated with the story of the Tower of Babel, in which men are determined to make themselves a name by the building of a 'city and a tower whose top may reach unto heaven' (Gen. 11.1-9). The growth of civilization, therefore, is accompanied by a degeneration of the spirit of man, caused by the human refusal to accept the conditions of creation.

Are we to assume that those who compiled and rewrote these early oral traditions with this view of human history in mind had no answer to the distressing problem which they raised? It is entirely likely that the creation and patriarchal traditions once were circulated independently. But the J writer has brought them together, and following the Tower of Babel story we are immediately informed of the election of Abraham. Considering the coherent nature of the J presentation, it is impossible to assume that the two are unrelated. Indeed, the only logical assumption is that the election of Israel in some way must be the answer to the plight of man. Second Isaiah, therefore, is elaborating and deepening no newly invented doctrine, when he proclaims:

> 'Thus saith the God, Yahweh,
> Who created the heavens and stretched them out,
> Who spread out the earth and its offspring,
> Who hast given breath to the people upon it,
> And spirit to those who walk on it:
> I am Yahweh;
> I have called thee in righteousness;
> I have taken hold of thy hand;
> I have preserved you and given you
> For a covenant of the people,
> For a light of the nations,
> For opening the eyes of the blind,
> For bringing out prisoners from the dungeon,
> From jail those who sit in darkness."
>
> (Isa. 42:5-7)

Israel's doctrine of a special election, therefore, was not quite what Celsus imagined it to be. The freedom and privilege which the election conferred were limited by the independent purposes of God. At least as early as the tenth or ninth centuries Israel's oral traditions were collected and rewritten to provide a viewpoint by which all history was comprehended. At the center of this history God had placed Israel and conferred upon her a responsibility coextensive with the privileges given. Precisely how God was to use Israel for the re-creation of the fallen world is a question for which the Old Testament presents no unified answer.[14] By no means all of the writers see *clearly* the universal aim of God or the mission of Israel for the saving of the nations. Yet all were conscious of a deep sense of responsibility. As God's peculiar possession, Israel had imposed upon her an obligation which to keep is life but to violate is disaster. Her election was not unalterable; it could be annulled by her own acts. The method employed to express this peculiar combination of privilege, obligation, and brittleness in election was the use of a particular vocabulary, drawn from the realm of jurisprudence. To this vocabulary we must now turn.

III

The doctrine of election found its most concrete expression in the Old Testament language of the covenant. This term was borrowed from the realm of law and given a special theological application. In nomadic or patriarchal society covenants between men and groups were the legal agreements or treaties which made peaceful community relations a possibility. Two familiar examples of such covenants are those between David and Jonathan (1 Sam. 18.3, 20.8, 23.18) and between Jacob and Laban (Gen. 31.44-55). In the latter the covenantal rite con-

[14] For a convenient review of some of the most important evidence see H. H. Rowley, *The Missionary Message of the Old Testament*, (London, Introduction dated 1944), chaps. II-IV. Cf. also W. J. Phythian-Adams, *The Call of Israel*, (London, 1934), Parts I and II.

sisted of the erection of a pillar or heap of stones, mutual vows, sacrificial offering, and community meal. The third party (or parties) of the agreement was (or were) the God of Abraham and the God of Nahor (v. 53), who made the covenant absolutely binding. In this connection we may observe that the early Hebrew and Amorite proper names portray the close relationship existing between a patriarchal group and its God; the latter was 'an actual member of the clan and could be addressed by a mortal kinsman as "father, brother," and even as "kindred." All members of the clan were, accordingly, children, brethren, or kinsmen of the god, who was head of the house,'[15] and who, we may add, was also a party to the clan's covenants.[16]

From this background in the social life the term was borrowed by Israel for a unique and unparalleled usage. That was to express the nature of the special relation existing between God and Israel. In this case covenant is no longer a legal compact between human beings, but a device for explaining the meaning and nature of Israel's election.[17] What was involved may perhaps be made clear by a brief reference to some of the covenant ceremonies.

The great post-exilic renewal of the covenant was a ceremony

[15] Albright, *From the Stone Age to Christianity*, p. 187.

[16] For the significance of the term 'covenant' in patriarchal society, see especially J. Pedersen, *Israel,* I-II (Oxford, 1926), pp. 279 ff., 308 ff., 414 ff., etc.

[17] So important was this conception of the covenant that W. Eichrodt in the first volume of his great work, *Theologie des Alten Testaments* (Leipzig, 1933) is enabled, in my opinion successfully, to reconstruct the whole theology of the Old Testament around it. One must agree, however, with K. Galling (*Die Erwählungstraditionen Israels,* p. 37) and H. Wheeler Robinson (*Inspiration and Revelation in the Old Testament,* p. 153) that the importance of covenant is primarily one of formal expression rather than of independent idea. It cannot be treated independently of election, because it merely puts into concrete terms, almost metaphorically, the meaning of the relationship involved in election. It is not in itself a redemptive act, but the expression and confirmation of this act.

which covered eight days (Neh. 8-10). During the first seven days Ezra read from 'the book of the law of Moses' (presumably in this case the complete Pentateuch), and a group of priests and Levites expounded it so that the people understood the meaning of what they heard (Neh. 8.7-8).[18] This was followed by a solemn public confession of sin and a formal resolve to keep the law, which was officially sealed for the people by both the political and religious leaders (Neh. 9.38).

In 621 B.C. the reform of Josiah was inaugurated by an official assembly, before which the king read 'the book of the covenant' (in this case some portion, at least, of the present Book of Deuteronomy). In the people's behalf he then is said to have 'made a covenant before Yahweh' to keep the law of Yahweh which he had just read (2 Kings 23.1-3).

During the ninth century in Judah, after the daughter of Jezebel, Athaliah, had been slain, we are informed that the chief priest, Jehoiada, 'made a covenant between himself, and all the people, and the king, that they should be Yahweh's people.' After that, the people destroyed the paraphernalia of the Baal cultus which Athaliah had introduced, re-established the temple service according to the law, and 'set the king on the throne of the kingdom' (2 Chron. 23.16-21).

In Joshua 24 the E document preserves a record of a covenant ceremony which took place at Shechem after the conclusion of the Conquest.[19] Following a review of God's dealings with Israel since the time of Abraham, Joshua presents the people with a direct challenge: 'Choose you this day whom ye will serve' (v. 15). When the people say they will serve Yahweh, Joshua gives solemn warning regarding the nature of the affirmation they are making. The people formally attest that they are witnesses to the oath they are taking and promise to put

[18] For the significance of such exposition in understanding the form of literature to which Deuteronomy and the Holiness Code of Lev. 17-26 belong, see G. von Rad, *Deuteronomium-Studien,* (Göttingen, 1947), pp. 7-24.

[19] Cf. also Deut. 27 and Joshua 8.30-35.

away the 'foreign gods' in their midst. So, it is said, 'Joshua made a covenant with the people that day' (v. 25).[20]

The Book of Deuteronomy preserves the tradition of a covenant ceremony in Moab in which the law was expounded by Moses and the people solemnly urged to keep it. In this case, however, it is made clear that this ceremony was one of rededication, a renewal of the Sinai covenant (see especially Chap. 29). In fact, the more we study the sources, the more we are led to Sinai for the original and normative compact between God and people. It was to this period that the origin of Israelite law was traced. In searching for the ideal pattern of true life, the prophets, the Deuteronomists, and the Priestly writers turned, not to the golden age of political, cultural and economic security under David and Solomon, but to the period of the wilderness wanderings, and to Sinai in particular. There the simplicity of relation between God and his Chosen People was most clearly seen, and there was found the origin of Israel's basic institutions.

The ceremony of ratification of the Sinai covenant is preserved in Exodus 24.1-8.[21] Here again the law was read (in

[20] The historical significance of this covenant in relation to the Sinai covenant is much debated. To this writer the views of Martin Noth are the most satisfactory (*Das Buch Josua*, Tübingen, 1938, pp. 108 f.; and *Das System der zwölf Stämme Israels*, Stuttgart, 1930, pp. 67 ff.). This scholar believes that Joshua 24, while it has been edited by the Deuteronomist, is an authentic, pre-Deuteronomic tradition relating to the Conquest of Canaan. Historically, it is concerned with the extension of the Sinai covenant to the complete amphictyony of twelve tribes which had come into being under Joshua's leadership. Certain of the tribes which had not been at Sinai here accept the covenant vows and tradition of those who had been there. In this way the sacral amphictyony of all twelve tribes in covenant around a central sanctuary came into being. From the standpoint of literary criticism Noth does not believe that this chapter has anything to do with the E document of Gen., Ex., and Num. Yet conceptual patterns and actual phraseology of the two are so close that one must at least assume that both were transmitted by the same circle in North Israel.

[21] These verses belong to the JE corpus of material; vs. 3-8 are usually assigned to E. It has sometimes been questioned as to whether J knew

this case 'the book of the covenant'), and the people replied: 'all that Yahweh hath spoken will we do and be obedient.' The sealing of the compact was by 'the blood of the covenant,' one part sprinkled on the altar and the other on the people.

Covenant, then, involved an interpretation of the meaning and aim of Israel's existence. Yahweh was primarily conceived under the metaphor of 'Lord' or Ruler who freely offered this compact. He did not impose it, but out of grace he offered it. The advantages were great, because acceptance meant the bestowal of blessing[22] from Yahweh, a blessing which included the gift of an 'inheritance,' security from enemies, law and order—indeed the wholesome and harmonious existence comprehended by the Biblical conception of peace (*shalom*).[23] Israel on her part freely accepted the covenant, but in doing so solemnly placed herself under obligation to obey the Ruler and the law which he gave as the constitution of the society. The covenant, therefore, placed the law in the center of the people's attention. Neither covenant nor law, however, were viewed primarily as a legal burden to be borne. They were founded in a Divine act of grace; they were God's gift of life. The Lord's 'Thou shalt' in the law broke through the collectivism of primitive man and imposed in the covenant an unconditional obedience, not only on the group, but on the individual as well.

of the covenant at all. Yet Ex. 34.10 and the whole implication of the J material involves the covenant quite as much as does E, though it is probable that most of the J account of the ceremony has been set aside in favor of the E narrative. See Carpenter and Harford, *The Composition of the Hexateuch* (London, 1902), p. 182 ff.; Driver, *Exodus* (Cambridge, 1911), pp. xxvii f., 168 ff.; Eissfeldt, *Einleitung in das Alte Testament* (Tübingen, 1934), p. 223; and especially G. von Rad, op. cit., pp. 13 ff. Contrast the views of Pfeiffer, *Introduction to the Old Testament* (New York, 1941), pp. 145 f.

[22] For the meaning and significance of this term, see Pedersen, *Israel* I-II, pp. 182 ff.

[23] *Ibid.*, pp. 263 ff., 311 ff.; and the writer's *Challenge of Israel's Faith* (Chicago, 1944, London, 1946), pp. 76 ff.

Yet the 'Thou shalt' was not arbitrary; it was God's gift that man might have life.[24]

In Israel, therefore, the social order was not grounded in nature, nor was the law a natural law. Law and society were brought into being through a special revelation of God in the setting of the covenant. A formless enslaved people who had no law were made into a nation and given a law. Consequently, Israel could rejoice in the law, for behind it lay the Giver, the redemptive God, who had set his love on a defenceless people for whom justice had been denied. As a result, the emphasis in Israel on the equality of all persons in the law, while not unknown elsewhere,[25] possessed overtones which were increasingly emphasized as time passed. The poor, the weak, and the defenceless received a consideration unknown elsewhere. In the Old Testament alone there was a complete prohibition against the taking of interest on a loan, because a poor man's need must not be the means for the enrichment of another. When the poor man cries unto God, says the Book of the Covenant (Ex. 22.27), God will hear for he is gracious. In that ancient world slavery was widely practised and was known also in Israel. Yet in Israel alone there was shown an interest in the victims of this system, and it was Israel which for the first time registered 'an open denial of the right of man to own man in perpetuity. This denial of the right of possession of man by man is as yet restricted to Hebrews only (cf. Neh. 5.8), but it is a step which no other religion had taken before.'[26] We note in this connection the statement of Job: 'Did not he that made

[24] Cf. W. Eichrodt, *Das Menschenverständnis des Alten Testaments* (Basel, 1944), pp. 7 ff.

[25] E.g. the passage in the Ugaritic legend of Keret (II Keret 6: 41-54; see *Syria*, Vol. XXIII, 1942-3, p. 12), in which the king is exhorted to 'judge the cause of the widow . . ., deliver the poor man . . ., feed the fatherless'; cf. H. L. Ginsberg, *Biblical Archaeologist*, Vol. VIII (1945), No. 2, p. 50.

[26] I. Mendelsohn, 'Slavery in the Ancient Near East,' *Biblical Archaeologist*, Vol. IX (1946), No. 4, p. 88. For excellent treatments of the social law of the Old Testament, see especially B. Balscheit and

me in the womb make him (the slave), and did not one fashion us in the womb? ' (Job 31.15). The prophetic protest against social injustice is without close parallel in the ancient world, and it was a protest grounded in a known law which the powerful were able to subvert by means of legal technicalities.

The justice and righteousness of God, therefore, were seen to be especially solicitous of the weak. They were a terror to the rich and the wicked, but a source of joy to the oppressed. Thus, the righteousness and grace of God were united in a way unknown elsewhere, and the term 'righteousness' could be used as a synonym for 'salvation.'[27] This peculiar combination of justice and mercy in God is especially developed in the Apostle Paul's treatment of the 'righteousness of God' (e.g. Rom. 1-3). It is a phenomenon peculiarly Biblical. Other religions, Zoroastrianism and Mohammedanism for example, know of the Divine power, holiness and goodness. But a righteousness that loves the weak and the outcast, a mercy in righteousness directed toward those whom the world's justice passes by—that is phenomenal and unique. It arose in the peculiar nature of the covenant law of Israel, given by God to the Chosen People; and it was that quality in God which transformed holiness from the non-moral to the moral, from fickle power to redemptive energy.

IV

Literary criticism has shown a tendency to regard the covenant doctrine as a fairly late invention in Israelite religious history, finding its first elaborate expression in the Deuteronomic literature of the seventh century.[28] In early Israel the relation-

W. Eichrodt, *Die soziale Botschaft des alten Testaments für die Gegenwart* (Basel, n.d.); and W. Eichrodt, *Was sagt das Alte Testament zum sozialen Leben* (Tübingen, 1948).

[27] Especially in Second Isaiah (cf. Isa. 45.8, 46.13, 51.5). Note also, however, such passages as Isa. 11.4-5; Jer. 23.6, 33.15-16; Hos. 2.19; Mal. 4.2.

[28] Cf. Wellhausen, *Prolegomena to the History of Israel*, translated

ship between Yahweh and people has been assumed to be a purely national one with little to distinguish it from the relation which existed between Chemosh and the people of Moab. The ground has been cut from under this view, however, by those German scholars who have been going beyond the methods of purely literary criticism to a criticism based on the history of tradition. Albrecht Alt and Martin Noth have shown without question that the early, pre-monarchial organization of Israel was utterly different from that of other contemporary people.[29] Before the time of Saul, Israel did not have a monarchial form of government. Instead there was an amphictyony, a league of tribes organized by compact around a central sanctuary. When in the Deuteronomic reform of 621 B.C. (2 Kings 22-23) and in the post-exilic community the ideal of a central sanctuary to the exclusion of all other sanctuaries was imposed, we may not infer that the conception was a new invention, as Wellhausen had supposed.[30] It was an honest attempt to recreate the sim-

from the German by J. S. Black and A. Menzies (Edinburgh, 1885), pp. 417 ff. The view is still retained by Pfeiffer, *Introduction to the Old Testament* (New York, 1941,), pp. 52, 198, 551. W. A. Irwin believes that, while the notion of covenant between God and Israel was first introduced in J and E, Hosea was the first to make specific mention of it (Hos. 6.7 and 8.1 are, he believes, the two genuine allusions to it in the eighth century). It was adopted by Jeremiah, and in Deuteronomy 'became an essential element of Israel's theology.' Irwin, following the critical line of reasoning current since the time of Wellhausen, regards 'the relation of Yahweh to the scattered tribes of the Judges' time . . . purely that of the national god. There is no reason to postulate any essential difference at this time between the attitude of Israel to her god and that of Moab or Ammon or Edom or any other nation to Chemosh, Milcom, or whatever appropriate deity' (*Intellectual Adventure of Ancient Man,* pp. 328 f.). Such references can easily be multiplied, though the surprising fact is that in the history-of-religion school of Old Testament scholarship little serious attention has been given the question.

[29] See especially Alt, *Die Staatenbildung der Israeliten in Palästina* (Leipzig, 1930) and Noth, *Das System der zwölf Stämme Israels* (Stuttgart, 1930).

[30] Cf. Wellhausen, *op. cit.*, pp. 17 ff.

plicity of the wilderness period. Deuteronomy with its lucid expression of the covenant theology can no longer be viewed as a pious forgery of the seventh century. While expanded and edited, its fundamental traditions were derived from the old amphictyonic circles in North Israel, as G. von Rad has recently proved.[31]

There is of course no way of showing that the word 'covenant' was used as early as the thirteenth or twelfth centuries. But there no longer can be any doubt that the election of Israel was given concrete expression in terms of a legal compact in the wilderness period. This does not mean that all of the tribes of Israel were originally included in the amphictyony.[32] Yet at a very early period most, if not all, of them joined the compact, accepting the Sinai tradition as normative. The covenant at Shechem, described in Josh. 24, may well have been the ceremony in which this took place.[33]

The all-pervading sense of election and covenant, therefore, is the chief clue for the understanding of Israel's sense of

[31] *Deuteronium-Studien* (Göttingen, 1947). Cf. also Adam Welch, *The Code of Deuteronomy* (London, 1924).

[32] For the difficulties in assuming an Exodus of all twelve tribes from Egypt, particularly in the light of present archaeological information, see the writer's review in *Westminster Historical Atlas to the Bible* (Philadelphia, 1945, London, 1947), pp. 33-40, and his remarks in 'The Present State of Biblical Archaeology,' *The Study of the Bible To-day and To-morrow,* edited by H. R. Willoughby (Chicago, 1947), pp. 83 ff. with references there cited.

[33] See note 20. As was the case with election, all sources regard the Sinai covenant as the fulfilment of the compact which God had made with Abraham. J and E describe the covenant with Abraham in Gen. 15. For the Deuteronomic conception, see Deut. 7.8 and 9.5. The Priestly editor of Genesis and Exodus has a scheme of history based on the idea of covenant. As election narrowed, a covenant was seen as concluding each stage of the history. The first was the covenant with Noah, the sign or token of which was the rainbow (Gen. 9.1-17). The second was the covenant with Abraham, its sign was the rite of circumcision (Gen. 17.1-14). Finally, according to P, the Mosaic covenant at Sinai was the climax of history. The Holy God had now condescended to 'tabernacle' (for a brief treatment of the meaning and significance of

destiny and of the meaning of existence. In other countries of the day, as far as we have knowledge, there was no comparable conception. The integration of the divine and human worlds was accomplished in a different way. Professor Henri Frankfort in his exceedingly important work, *Kingship and the Gods* (Chicago, 1948), has shown that in Egypt and Mesopotamia the office of the king was the institution which integrated society, which served as the mediator between the gods and men, and which harmonized the life of the community with the natural world. In Egypt the Pharaoh was a god incarnate, through whom all blessing was channeled to the people. The government was a vast paternalistic bureaucracy of delegated powers, the extension of the authority of the god at the head, who as a participator in the world of the divine freed the people from fear and uncertainty. Freedom was sacrificed for a never-changing integration of society and nature. In Mesopotamia the king was the appointee, the servant, the son of the gods. Deification was not a central motive; the king was a human being, appointed and adopted by the gods.[34] Yet he like the Pharaoh was charged with the task of maintaining the social order in harmony with nature and the divine.

In Israel, too, once the office of monarchy was established, the king was conceived as chosen by Yahweh and could even be spoken of as Yahweh's 'son' (e.g. 2 Sam. 7.14). In certain of the Psalms it is said that Yahweh will give the king victory over all enemies, and thus the people will have security, The

this term, see Frank M. Cross, Jr., 'The Tabernacle,' *Biblical Archaeologist*, Vol. X, 1947, No. 3, especially pp. 65 ff.) in the people's midst. The sign or token of this covenant was, as Frank M. Cross, Jr., has pointed out to me, the Sabbath (Ex. 6.2-8, 29.43-45, 31.12-17).

[34] In the opinion of this writer the work of Frankfort shows the one-sided and superficial nature of I. Engnell's work, *Studies in Divine Kingship in the Ancient Near East* (Uppsala, 1943). Engnell finds the conception of the divine-king throughout the Near East, and fails completely to make those careful distinctions which one must make in dealing with different cultures: see the criticisms of Frankfort, *Kingship* . . ., p. 405, note 1, and T. H. Gaster, *Review of Religion,*

king will give justice, destroy the wicked, provide the poor and the needy with judgment, and thus preserve the social order. Psalm 89 speaks of the Davidic king as ' chosen out of the people ' (v. 19), as Yahweh's anointed servant (v. 20), whom Yahweh will strengthen, defeat his enemies (vv. 21-25), follow with faithfulness and loyalty (*hesed*). He will call God ' father,' and God will make him his first-born, ' higher than the kings of the earth ' (v. 27). With him God has made a covenant so that his throne shall endure ' as the days of heaven.' If the people break God's law they will be punished; but God has not lied to David; he will not break the covenant with him (vv. 28-35).[35]

The Israelite king like most Mesopotamian kings was not deified. He was adopted as God's son or anointed (Messiah) to protect the people from their enemies and to secure the social order in righteousness.[36] A theology of kingship evidently arose in the court circles of Jerusalem, out of which the conception of the future Messiah naturally grew. When current kings betrayed their trust, God, it was believed, would raise up an Anointed One who would fulfil the theological conditions on which the monarchy rested. The dividing line between the historical and the eschatological conceptions of kingship is thus

Vol. IX (1944-5), pp. 267 ff. That certain kings in Mesopotamia at times claimed some sort of fusion with a deity seems not to be denied, but such claims were exceptions to the otherwise dominant pattern of appointee or servant. This much must at least be admitted even by those who reject Frankfort's treatment of the matter in his Chap. 21.

[35] For Psalms which directly relate to the earthly king, cf. numbers 20, 21, 45, 61, 72, 89, 101, 110, 132, etc. Cf. also J. Pedersen, *Israel* III-IV (London, 1940), pp. 77 ff.

[36] Psalm 45.6 (Hebrew 7) is the only instance where the king is addressed as ' god ' (*'elohim*), unless we include also the Messianic passage, Isa. 9.6 (Hebrew 5) where the Messianic king is called ' Mighty God ' (*'el gibbor*). These passages, however, cannot be used to establish an Israelite divine-king in view of the manifold evidence for the contrary view. They must be interpreted as due more to an exaggerated exuberance upon the part of the authors than to a seasoned and reasoned theology of divine kingship.

very difficult, if not impossible, to draw; the second was simply the extension of the first to the age of God's fulfilment of his covenanted promises.

A Scandinavian group of scholars has for some time been intensely interested in the theology of the Israelite kingship. They believe it to have been essentially the same as that held in the different theological environment of Canaan and Mesopotamia. Most of the Psalms are interpreted as cultic poems, used in the great New Year's festival, when as in Babylon the Israelite king re-enacted the part of the divine king of the gods who at the dawn of history fought and won the battle for creation against chaos. He also took the part of the dying-rising storm or vegetation deity in the cultic drama which secured for the state the blessings of earth for the coming year. The suffering servant of Isa. 53 is interpreted in this light. The 'I' of the Psalms is believed, for the most part, to be the king. The phrase 'to David' in the titles of many of the Psalms is interpreted as having nothing to do with authorship but as an old cultic-liturgical rubric meaning 'a psalm for the king.' Kingship, especially as it re-enacts the divine battle drama each year, is seen by these scholars to have been a central, if not *the* central factor, in Israelite life, providing that integrating security with nature and the cosmos which gave meaning to life and protection from trouble. If all this is true, then Israel differed little from her environment in the most vital aspect of her faith, that having to do with the meaning, the establishment, and the perpetuation of the social order.[37]

[37] See Engnell, *op. cit.*, especially pp. 174 ff. and 'The Ebed Yahweh Songs and the Suffering Messiah in "Deutero-Isaiah",' *Bulletin of the John Rylands Library*, Vol. 31 (1948), pp. 3 ff.; A. Bentzen, *Messias-Moses redivivus-Menschensohn* (Zürich, 1948); 'The Cultic Use of the Story of the Ark in Samuel,' *Journal of Biblical Literature*, Vol. LXVII (1948), pp. 37 ff.; 'On the Ideas of "the old" and "the new" in Deutero-Isaiah,' *Studia Theologica*, Vol. I (1947), pp. 183 ff. Pedersen, *op. cit.*, pp. 428 ff., 746 ff. Bentzen and especially Pedersen are far more cautious than Engnell, who seems to be engaged in a single-minded search for the divine-king *motif* in the Old Testament with the

While the Scandinavian scholars have thrown considerable light on the theology of the monarchy and of the Messiah in Israel, certain qualifications must be made. The initial assumption that virtually all of the Psalms and much other Old Testament literature were composed as ritual material for use in the cult cannot be proved. Still less can it be proved that there was ever an important cult drama in Israel each New Year's Day in which a divine battle myth, borrowed from Canaan or Babylon, was re-enacted with the king taking the role of the victorious God. Certainly none of the Old Testament ritual preserved, including that of the Day of Atonement, contains any hint of such a drama. We shall return to this subject in the next chapter, though here it may be said that cultic re-enactment of myth, based upon elements of sympathetic magic, is completely foreign to Israelite worship.

Even more important is the relationship between the Davidic covenant and the Sinai covenant. As Frankfort has pointed out so clearly, Israelite kingship does indeed conform in important respects to other Near Eastern types, but this, like other borrowed features in Hebrew culture, is least significant. In the case of kingship, the borrowing has to do with 'externalities, the less important since they did not affect the basic oddness of the Hebrew institution. If kingship counted in Egypt as a function of the gods, and in Mesopotamia as a divinely ordained political order, the Hebrews knew that they had introduced it on their own initiative, in imitation of others and under the strain of emergency' (cf. 1 Sam. 8.19-20).[38]

Even after a theology of kingship was established during and after the days of David and Solomon, normative Yahwism continued to point to the kingless period of the wilderness as the formative and normative phase of Israelite culture. The

result that other more important factors in Israelite religious life are not seen in their correct proportion. See further Chap. I, note 32, Chap. III, Sect. II, and Elmer A. Leslie, *The Psalms* (New York and Nashville, 1949), pp. 62 ff.

[38] Frankfort, *Kingship and the Gods*, p. 339.

covenant with David was parallel to, but never replaced and never attained a standing in most Israelite circles equal to that of the covenant at Sinai. Undoubtedly, some in the royal court tried to make it so, if we may judge from certain of the Psalms. Yet they never succeeded completely, because the people had a prior association with Yahweh as the true king and an original constitution which was held normative even for the king. Hammurabi of Babylon was given the law for the country by the divine judge, Shamash. But in Israel the law was prior to kingship, and was given in connection with the covenant to the whole people. The king could claim no credit for it; he could only administer it. Frankfort puts the matter succinctly:

> Nowhere else in the Near East do we find this dissociation of a people from its leader in relation to the divine; with the Hebrews we find parallelism while everywhere else we find coincidence. In the meager information about Hebrew ritual it has been attempted to find indications that the king fulfilled a function not unlike that of contemporary rulers. But even if we take an exceptional and apparently simple phrase, '(Solomon) sat on the throne of the Lord as king, instead of David, his father' (1 Chron. 29.23), we need only compare this with the corresponding phrases 'throne of Horus' or 'throne of Atum' to realize that the Hebrew expression can only mean 'throne favored by the Lord' or something similar. The phrase confirms what the account of Saul's elevation and David's scruples showed in the first place—namely, that there was a connection between the king's person and sanctity, as there was a connection between the king's fate and national destiny. But these relations were not the nerve center of the monarchy, as they were in Egypt and Mesopotamia, but rather cross-currents due to the religious orientation of Hebrew society; and their secondary nature stands out most clearly when we consider the functions of the Hebrew king.[39]

Hebrew kingship, therefore, never achieved the sanctity or the absolutism which is encountered elsewhere. The office of the prophet, the herald of Yahweh, was independent of king-

[39] *Ibid.*, pp. 341 f.

ship and was therefore free to enter into open conflict with the monarchy.[40] The conception of Yahweh as the covenant-Lord of Israel, the Chosen People, prevented the Israelite monarchy from presuming too much and left independent religious leaders free to pronounce judgment on the kings for doing evil in the sight of Yahweh. It also permitted a people of Yahweh to survive destruction and exile, and attempt to rebuild a holy community without a king in the light of the wilderness period. In the words of Frankfort again:

> The keeping of Yahweh's covenant meant relinquishing a great deal. It meant, in a word, sacrificing the greatest good ancient Near Eastern religion could bestow—the harmonious integration of man's life with the life of nature. . . . It excluded, in particular, the king's being instrumental in the integration of society and nature. . . . To Hebrew thought nature appeared void of divinity, and it was worse than futile to seek a harmony with created life when only obedience to the will of the Creator could bring peace and salvation. . . . In Hebrew religion—and in Hebrew religion alone—the ancient bond between man and nature was destroyed.[41]

V

The doctrine of election and covenant gave Israel an interpretation of life and a view of human history which are absolutely fundamental to Christian theology, especially when they are seen with Christ as their fulfilment.

The sense of the goodness and meaningfulness of life and of the true nature of personality were achieved in a context of communion, interdependence and relatedness. The worth of

[40] The priesthood was in a different situation. The chief priest or priests of the Jerusalem temple were members of the royal administrative cabinet (cf. 2 Sam. 8.17; 1 Kings 4.4). As a result they were a support for the *status quo,* and rarely if ever were a dynamic force for social change during the time of the monarchy. Cf. Albright, *Archæology and the Religion of Israel,* pp. 107 ff., 138 f.

[41] Frankfort, *ibid*., pp. 342 f.

man was seen, not so much as a natural possession or right, as it was a right conferred by or derived from God. Personality achieved its true depth and stature in a relation of faith, love and unqualified obedience to God. God has set his love on man and man was to respond in gratitude with a sense of imperative obligation. The problem of life was analysed, therefore, not over against nature and the question of security within it, but in the much deeper relation with the will of God who created nature and called society into being. Primary attention was accordingly focused on the problem of the will. The will of man in relation to the will of God was the central problem of existence.

The real heroes of the Bible, then, were heroes of faith, whose claim to greatness lay in their response to the call of God. The election of Israel held within it the election also of the individual. The type of law, peculiar to Israel and not to be found elsewhere in the ancient world, was that of the 'Thou shalt,' or apodictic, tradition.[42] In the covenant with the whole people Yahweh's 'Thou shalt' was addressed directly to each individual, singling him out of the mass and demanding of him an individual response not comprehended in the cultic activity of the group as a whole. Individual and corporate responsibility, therefore, went hand in hand. The popular notion to-day that individualism did not emerge in Israel until the time of Jeremiah and Ezekiel is a judgment based upon an inadequate comprehension of the data. In the earliest law of the covenant the individual is addressed together with the group, and life achieved its true meaning in the context of God's promise and demand, and of man's faith and obedience.[43]

Furthermore, this sense of relatedness and obligation furnished the means by which the events of life were to be interpreted. The alternation of success and failure, of joy and hate,

[42] See A. Alt, *Die Ursprünge des israelitischen Rechts* (Leipzig, 1934).

[43] This subject is well analysed in the work of W. Eichrodt, *Das Menschenverständnis des Alten Testaments* (Basel, 1944); cf. also his *Theologie des Alten Testaments*, Vol. III (Leipzig, 1939), pp. 1-18.

of happiness and unhappiness, of peace and war, of security and insecurity, could only be understood in relation to God's promise of blessing and cursing, grace and judgment, love and wrath. The nature of God's activity at any immediate moment was conditioned by the nature of man's response. Thus a profound conception of sin as rebellion against God and a breach of the covenant came into being. To this rebellion God's response was one of punishment. Yet a thoroughgoing repentance usually meant that God would also 'repent': i.e. he would not then do what previously he had said he would do when the people were in sin. This living relation of man with God in the covenant, then, focused attention on sin, repentance, and forgiveness in a manner and in a depth entirely unknown elsewhere.

Of course, the passing of the centuries brought a deepening in the understanding of these realities of the spirit. Israel's theological vocabulary became more penetrating and extensive, especially in the prophets. But the development was one which took place within the covenant, not outside it. Things basically or entirely new were not added by the prophets, except as new events made necessary a deeper understanding of the implications of the covenant.[44] The course of the centuries brought increasing complexity into the social life, and the clash of empires brought a succession of crises in which Israel was involved. The Prophetic, Deuteronomic, and Priestly writings are pervaded by a somber, almost overwhelming sense of sin and judgment. With a deep seriousness and a touch of nostalgia they turned back to the wilderness period to rediscover the bases upon which the national life was established. Beyond that was also the wonder of God's creative acts at the beginning

[44] Contrast N. H. Snaith, *The Distinctive Ideas of the Old Testament* (London, 1944; and Philadelphia, 1946), who finds the prophets to be the authors of 'the first truly distinctive development among the Hebrews' (p. 51 in British Edition). Cf., however, the excellent essay by John Bright, 'The Prophets were Protestants,' in *Interpretation,* Vol. I (1947), pp. 153 ff.

of time. Yet so confident were they of the reliability of God's election promises that they looked to the future for their fulfilment. Creation and election, promise and fulfilment, were the means by which history was interpreted.[45]

Thus it came about that the Biblical sense of history was born. The contemporary polytheisms, having analysed the problem of life over against nature, had little sense of or concern with the significance of history. Nature with its changing seasons was cyclical, and human life, constantly integrating itself with nature by means of cultic activity and sympathetic magic, moved with nature in a cyclical manner. But Israel was little interested in nature, except as God used it together with his historical acts to reveal himself and to accomplish his purpose. Yahweh was the God of history, the living God unaffected by the cycles of nature, who had set himself to accomplish a definite purpose in time. Consequently, the religious literature of Israel was primarily concerned with the history of God's acts in and through his Chosen People. The great confessions of faith were primarily historical reviews of what God had done and what the people had done in response.[46] Their purpose was to engender faith, praise, and repentance. The story of the past was the guide to the present and the key to the future. Both beginning and end, creation and eschatology, therefore, became an integral part of the Israelite view of time.

This sense of the movement of history toward a future goal, in which the promises of the past and the hopes of the present find their fulfilment, is the source of our modern conception

[45] Cf. the excellent analysis of W. Eichrodt, 'Offenbarung und Geschichte im Alten Testament,' *Theologische Zeitschrift,* 4. Jahrgang, Heft 5 (Sept.-Okt., 1948), pp. 321-331.

[46] Cf., for example, Deut. 1-4, 32; Josh. 24; 2 Sam. 22; Ps. 18; 1 Kings 8.15-26; Neh. 9.5-38; Ps. 78, 105, 106; etc. In the New Testament early Christian preaching was of the same order: cf. Acts 2.14 ff., 3.12 ff., 7.2-53, etc. (See C. H. Dodd, *The Apostolic Preaching and its Developments,* London, 1936).

of history in the Western world. Both liberal idealism and Marxism have, of course, secularized the Biblical conception, but both owe their genesis ultimately to this completely unique and revolutionary doctrine. Yet Israel could not have arrived at this awareness of the meaning of time apart from her theology of election. The God who had chosen her had a purpose in mind in doing so, and that purpose he would fulfil. Consequently, history is in movement toward a goal solely because God has determined both the movement and the goal.

To the modern historian it must appear extraordinary and amazing that such an interest in the activity of God should produce history. To-day, theology and history are separated. Objectivity is the basis of the science of history, and a theological bias is believed to mean its perversion.[47] Nevertheless the Christian historian may draw considerable measure of comfort from the Hebrew achievement. What Israelite men of faith accomplished may be summarized in these words of Professor James T. Shotwell in the first volume of his *The History of History*:[48]

> No higher tribute could be paid to the historical worth of the Old Testament than the statement that, when considered upon the profane basis of human authorship, it still remains one of the greatest products in the history of history, a record of national tradition, outlook, and aspiration, produced by a poor, harassed, semi-barbarous people torn by feud and swept by conquest, which yet retains the undying charm of genuine art and the universal appeal of human interest.

Quite apart from its importance in the history of history, the Old Testament continues to amaze the students of literature for the high quality of its artistry in historical narration and the purity and depth of the emotions it expressed in poetry. Egypt,

[47] Cf. the quotations on this point of view collected by H. G. Wood, *Christianity and the Nature of History* (Cambridge, 1934), pp. 110 ff.

[48] New York, 1939, p. 108.

Canaan, and Babylon possessed many models from which Israel learned and borrowed much. Yet it is universally conceded that the Old Testament far surpasses the literature produced in those centers of culture.[49] Is there a reason for this phenomenon, or are we simply to rest on an assertion of the Israelite literary genius? It appears to this writer that more should be said. Israelite theology involved such a concentration on history, that the art of narration was highly developed. In addition, that same theology exercised a purifying effect upon the mind, with the result that simplicity, straightforwardness, honesty, the purity of expression and emotion heightened by restraint—these and other literary qualities became an unconscious part of the Israelite's literary effort. In the Old Testament there is such a close interrelation existing between theological content and literary form that the two cannot be separated.

VI

Finally, in what sense can the Old Testament be considered revelation? The Christian is one who has committed himself; accordingly, he does not stand on neutral ground. For him the unique, the discontinuous, the extraordinary nature of the Old Testament can only be explained as the dramatic, purposeful intervention of God, who here was inaugurating a special revelation of himself, one which culminated in Christ. In the fields of law, politics, economics, literature, cultus, and even of the affective and conceptual life, Israel was heavily dependent upon and thoroughly a part of her environment. One, therefore, can single out point after point where the Old Testament was a part of its world. Yet the astonishing thing is that far more basic resemblances exist between the religions of the

[49] The literature on this subject is very large, but see especially, W. F. Albright, *Archaeology and the Religion of Israel*, Chap. I; T. E. Peet, *A Comparative Study of the Literatures of Egypt, Palestine, and Mesopotamia* (London, 1931).

ancient world than exist between the Bible and any one of them. What Israel borrowed was the least significant; it was fitted into an entirely new context of faith. What once was pagan now became thoroughly Israelite, or else became the source of dissension in the community. Consequently, the Christian and the Jew as well, look upon this distinctiveness of the Old Testament as proof of its claim for special revelation.

On the other hand, it has become customary to speak of Biblical faith as a revealed religion, and of other faiths as natural religion or religions of culture.[50] In what sense is the Old Testament to be fitted into such a differentiation? We certainly are not to think of the polytheisms as completely devoid of an interest in revelation. Polytheistic man was vitally and intensely concerned to learn the will of the gods. And the gods actually made known their will in special oracles of all kinds and especially in the establishment of the social order through the king and the maintenance of that order in harmony with nature. Dreams were an important source of revelation just as in Israel. Kings sought an oracle before entering battle just as did David and Ahab. The seriousness with which such oracles were sought is illustrated by the Mari letters. Three hundred Babylonian and three hundred Mari soldiers had gone on an expedition against an enemy caravan. Each section of the troops had its own diviner whose job was to assemble the omens. In another campaign considerable difficulty was experienced because the omens were not favorable.[51]

Yet in Israel the doctrine of election involved a view of a special and unique revelation of the nature and purpose of the

[50] Cf., e.g., H. Kraemer, *The Christian Message in a Non-Christian World* (London, 1938); N. Söderblom, *The Living God* (London and New York, 1933), and *The Nature of Revelation* (New York, 1933); John Baillie and Hugh Martin, editors, *Revelation* (London, 1937).

[51] G. E. Mendenhall, 'Mari,' *Biblical Archaeologist,* Vol. XI (1948), No. 1, p. 18.

true God, which was without parallel elsewhere. This revelation, furthermore, was not primarily in dreams or omens. The knowledge of God was something far greater than a specific answer to a specific question in an oracle. History was important and carefully examined because the true knowledge of God was there to be found. Consequently, once the history was rehearsed and written down, it was a basic source of reference for God's revelation of himself. The oracles spoken by the prophets as direct and immediate messages from God were fitted into the context of this history as the revelation of God's immediate and future action in the light of the consistent purpose he had demonstrated in the past.

Thus while Israel possessed direct oracles from God as did the polytheist from his gods, those oracles were an integral part of a continuous unfolding of a special activity of the sole divine Reality. They were not isolated, occasional, and unrelated utterances given in response to a question for the selfish benefit of the questioner. Such utterances are, of course, known in Israel, but they did not produce the Old Testament, nor did they reveal God's nature as did the history of the divine activity. It is scarcely an accident that natural religion, when its course is not interrupted, works itself out into philosophy or mysticism. Biblical faith has always resisted complete surrender to either.

In conclusion, it must be pointed out that the Old Testament as revelation has been found to be incomplete. It ended with an unfulfilled hope for completion. Thus, neither Judaism nor Christianity has been able to live in the Old Testament alone. In the conception of law as elaborated in the Talmud, Judaism has based its religion. The Talmud has actually received the primary attention because it is believed to summarize and to make relevant the faith of the fathers. Christianity, on the other hand, has seen the revelation to Israel completed in Christ. He has become the Head of a New Israel which continues the faith of the fathers as that faith is fulfilled by God's dramatic act in the death and resurrection of his Son. Christianity and Judaism, though they spring from the same source, are very different religious faiths, because they have seen the completion of an incomplete revelation accomplished in different ways.

CHAPTER THREE

'WHAT DOTH THE LORD THY GOD REQUIRE?'

A STUDY of the means by which the Divine is worshipped and served is a vast and complicated subject. Forms of worship are the most conservative elements in any culture, and the distinctiveness of a religion is often to be found, not so much in the particular forms, as in the spiritual attitudes which lie back of their use. Yet the historian of the past finds it easier to describe the outward acts than to discover inner attitudes, because the latter are hidden from us except as they find partial expression in the words of hymns and prayers.

To the modern Protestant, there are few more dry and unrewarding subjects than Israel's sacrificial cultus; we have been grateful that the early Church saw it fulfilled and completed in Jesus Christ so that we can leave consideration of it to those of the Catholic tradition in the Christian community who still preserve some continuity with it in their ritual![1] The worship of God by means of animal sacrifice was a practice taken over by Israel from her environment. So also were the ideas of tabernacle and temple, new moon and harvest festivals, clean and unclean or tabu, etc. It is small wonder, therefore, that scholars of the last few generations have found this aspect of

[1] It is the Anglo-Catholics who have recently shown most interest in the Priestly theology of the Old Testament: see, for example, the works of W. J. Phythian-Adams, particularly *The People and the Presence* (London and New York, 1942), and *The Way of At-one-ment* (London, 1944). Others of the free church tradition have read these books with great interest because they are dealing with matters they have neglected. Yet in doing so they become a bit uncomfortable because of the concentration on the Priestly over against the prophetic emphasis and because they suspect that the ulterior motive behind such works is to provide the theological background for a particular form of church government.

the religion of Israel a fertile source for comparative study and have concluded that before the eighth century prophets Israel had little that was distinctive. Yet if the assertions previously made concerning a unique theology even in early Israel are in any measure correct, then it would be very surprising if that theology had failed to have a decisive influence on the forms of worship. I think it can be shown that this was the case.

I

When we examine the world of polytheism more closely, we find beneath the surface a vast, dark, and uncomfortable world, comparable in its complexity to those depths of unconscious life laid bare by modern psychoanalysis. That is the world of demons, magic, and divination. By contrast, the first and most obvious thing which we can say about Israel is that, comparatively speaking, her religious life is most astonishingly free of this sort of thing, at least in ideal. Both the Israelite and the polytheist were most vitally concerned with the discovery of the divine will and with the proper service to be accorded to deity. But to the polytheist there was available a methodology for influencing nature and the gods from which Israel for the most part was excluded.

Magic seems to be based on a pre-logical conception of reality and identity which is foreign to the rational man's conception of cause and effect.[2] The *idea* of a table and the table are one and the same thing. The image of a god or a person which appears in a dream *is* that being. An effigy made to resemble a living object *is* that object. Stick a pin or needle through the image and the living being will die. In the history of my own seminary at least one professor is known to have been hung and burned in effigy. The ultimate background of that student prank lies in the primitive notion that actual

[2] Cf., e.g., Lucien Lévy-Bruhl, *How Natives Think* (London, 1926; translated by Lilian A. Clare), especially Chaps, II, VI-VIII.

physical harm can be done to a person by such symbolic activity.

The name and the word of another being cannot be separated from the reality. They produce pictures and impressions in the mind which are real. Consequently, the use of name and word in blessings and curses is effective. Since the stars and planets are manifestations of the gods, their movements and characteristics can be studied with great care for signs which have been correlated with human life. Our word 'lunacy' with the meaning of insanity, is a survival from a time when great powers were attributed to the moon; the mysterious powers of the zodiac and the whole cult of astrology originate in the same mental environment. Any and every abnormality in life may be a sign of some sort; elaborate and highly specialized techniques were devised to discover its meaning.

One of the earliest valuable historical sources for patriarchal Palestine is a number of potsherds from Egypt on which the names of Asiatic enemies were written, after which the pottery was smashed into pieces. In this way the enemies were thought to be easily defeated.[3] In a Canaanite epic from Ugarit in northern Syria a king named Keret is sick unto death. When the head of the divine pantheon, El, can find no god able to remove the sickness he exclaims: 'I will apply sorcery and will surely compass the removal of the illness, driving out the malady.'[4] Earlier in the same epic an obscure passage seems to say that Keret's children poured out oil and by sympathetic magic influenced Baal to rain upon the earth so that the crops

[3] For convenient summaries of the documents, see W. F. Albright, *Journal of the Palestine Oriental Society*, 1928, pp. 223 ff.; *Bulletin of the American Schools of Oriental Research*, No. 81 (Feb. 1941), pp. 16 ff., and No. 83 (Oct. 1941), pp. 30 ff., with references to the other literature on the subject.

[4] Ginsberg's translation of lines 25-28 of Col. 5 of section C (II K) of the Keret legend: see his *The Legend of King Keret* (*Bulletin of the American Schools of Oriental Research*, Supplementary Studies, Nos. 2-3, New Haven, 1946), p. 30. The root of the verb here translated 'sorcery' (*ḥarash*) is used as a noun, also with the meaning of magic, in Isa. 3.3.

might grow.[5] In the epic of Baal and Anat, the latter in revenge for the slaying of Baal by Mot (Death), attacks Mot, 'cutting him off with the sword, winnowing him with the sieve, burning him in the fire, grinding his ashes with the handmill, sowing what was left of him in the field, in order that birds might eat their portion, utterly destroying the sprouts.'[6] Albright writes[7]: 'No other mythology has so explicitly described the sympathetic ritual by which the god of grain is restored to life. The ritual was intended to revive Baal by sympathetic action, not to bring the god of death himself to life.'

It is from Mesopotamia, however, that our richest sources for the study of early magic and divination come. In almost every large collection of tablets found a number have to do with omens of various sorts. That is particularly true of the large library of Asshurbanapal, found a century ago in the ruins of Nineveh. Indeed, a majority of the tablets in that library are said to be concerned with magic and divination, particularly with astrology. No other people of the ancient world studied the movements of the stars and planets with greater care. In part, this concern was necessitated by the need for adjusting the calendar. And the achievements of Babylonian astronomers are surprising. One astronomer, for example, endeavored to determine the true date of the new or full moon with which was connected the determination of lunar and solar eclipses. His calculations on the diameter of the moon's face are said to be even more accurate than were the estimates of Ptolemy, Copernicus, or Kepler before the last-mentioned began to use the telescope.[8]

[5] *Ibid.*, p. 29 (Keret C, Col. 3).

[6] Albright's rendering in *Archæology and the Religion of Israel,* p. 86. The text is that numbered by Gordon as 49, section II, lines 31 ff. (See C. H. Gordon, *Ugaritic Handbook,* Rome, 1947, Vol. II, pp. 137 ff.; C. Virolleaud, *Syria* 12, 1931, pp. 193 ff.).

[7] Albright, *loc. cit.*

[8] George G. Cameron, *Biblical Archaeologist,* Vol. VII (1944), No. 2, p. 38.

Yet science and magic were interrelated, and the profession of deducing omens from the movements of the heavenly bodies reached such importance in the late Assyrian empire that a system of periodic reports to the king came into being. The following are a few examples chosen at random:

When Mars approaches the moon and stands, the moon will cause evil to inhabit the land. When a planet stands at the left horn of the moon, the king will act mightily. When Virgo stands at its left horn, in that year the vegetables of Akkad will prosper. . . . When Mars approaches Scorpio, the prince will die by a scorpion's sting, and his son after him will take the throne. . . . Last night there was an earthquake. When the earth quakes in (the month of) Tebet, the king will sit in the city of his foe. . . . When the earth quakes in the night, there will be harm to the land (or) devastation to the land. . . . On the fourteenth an eclipse will take place; it is evil for Elam and Akharru, lucky for the king, my lord; let the king, my lord, rest happy. . . . An eclipse has happened but it is not visible in Asshur. . . . The great gods in the city wherein the king dwells have obscured the heavens and will not show the eclipse; so let the king know that this eclipse is not directed against the king, my lord, or his country. Let the king rejoice.[9]

Far more common, especially among the people, was divination by a variety of humbler means, one of which was the inspection of the liver of animals. Clay models were made of the formation of the liver, so that a record might be preserved for study and reference. Ezekiel 21.21-22 portrays what must have been a typical ancient scene. The king of Babylon is pictured as standing at a parting of the way. One road leads to Rabbath, the Ammonite capital, the other to Jerusalem. To choose which way he should go he used divination. He shook the divining arrows in a quiver, consulted the deities whose images were with him, and looked at the liver of a sacrificial animal.

[9] R. Campbell Thompson, *The Reports of the Magicians and Astrologers of Nineveh and Babylon*, Vol. II (London, 1900); quoted are portions of texts Nos. 234, 239, 266, 273, 274.

The Babylonian diviner (*baru*) was so expert in his trade that he spread it throughout the Near East. The personal seal of one such diviner, who calls himself 'the servant of Ea,' was found in a thirteenth-century stratum at Beth-shan in Palestine.[10] Of the same age is the most famous of the class, the diviner Balaam, from northern Mesopotamia, hired by Balak, king of Moab, at considerable expense to curse Israel. Being unable or unwilling to do anything more effective, Balak tried to halt Israel by magical means, but the Israelite version of the story, preserved in Num. 22-24, takes delight in showing how Yahweh turned the divination to his own purposes.

It has been shown that the procedure followed by Balaam conformed to the ritual prescribed for the Mesopotamian diviner. On a certain morning Balaam had Balak prepare seven altars and offer seven sacrifices. Then Balak was told to stay by the sacrifices while Balaam determined the omen, that is, the divine word. Each detail of the action followed the rules of divination, even to the time of day, for best results were thought to be obtained in the morning before sunrise. But the first divination did not succeed, or at least the answer came out wrong as far as Balak was concerned. So they tried again at another place (Num. 23.13), but the omen was the same. A third attempt was made. Since the number three was important in Babylonian magic, Balak would not give up until they had tried again. But during the course of the third performance, Balaam suddenly gave up the divination (Chap. 24.1), perhaps for fear he might lose his reputation, and began to utter prophecies. The result, of course, was that Balak became so disgusted that he refused to pay Balaam the promised fee.[11]

[10] Alan Rowe, *The Topography and History of Beth-shan* (Philadelphia, 1930), p. 23 and Pl. 34.3.

[11] For a detailed analysis of the story in the light of the Babylonian divination, see S. Daiches, *Hilprecht Anniversary Volume* (Leipzig, 1909), pp. 60-70. Daiches, it would appear, has seen more clearly the original nature of the incident than A. Guillaume, *Prophecy and Divination* (New York and London, 1938), pp. 133 ff.

The story as related by the Israelite writers is told with high good humor, for to them it was absurd that Babylonian magic could do anything to thwart the purposes of the God of Israel. Indeed, God took the pagan specialist and made a prophet out of him for Israel's sake.

More disturbing, however, was the vast world of demonology. Sickness, strife, and trouble of every sort were usually believed to be caused by lesser deities who were pictured in the weirdest forms, possessing the most fantastic combinations of animal, bird, and human bodies. The Oriental Institute of the University of Chicago, for example, possesses an excellent bronze representation of Pazuzu, one of the cruellest sources of human misery. He was the demon of the southwest wind, 'king of the evil spirits of the air,' who 'rules the world quarters and devastates the pure mountains.'[12] The figure was probably made to insure the exact application of a charm or incantation uttered against him. For the chief weapons against such demons were magical spells, incantations, and prayers in the form of appeals to the great gods. Some of the prayers occasionally approach the beauty of the Hebrew penitential psalms, but it should not be forgotten that for the most part they were composed to be used in connection with the incantation rites of the priestly specialists in exorcism.[13]

An interesting example of Babylonian medicine in its combination of magic and actual therapeutic treatment is provided by an incantation written for people with toothache. It begins with the story of creation and the record of how the worm came into being. The worm, unsatisfied with the food offered it, wept before the great gods: 'Let me drink among the teeth, and set me on the gums, that I may devour the blood of the

[12] So Cameron, *op cit.*, Fig. 7.

[13] Cf. Guillaume, *op. cit.*, pp. 28 ff., and the treatment of the Babylonian prayers of 'The Lifting of the Hand' by L. W. King, *Babylonian Magic and Sorcery* (London, 1896).

teeth, and of their gums destroy their strength. Then shall I hold the bolt of the door.' Thus toothache came into being, and by reciting the story the magician shows that he possesses definite knowledge of his enemy, a fundamental requirement in magic. Now he may proceed with his spell: 'So must thou say this: "O Worm! May Ea smite thee with the might of his fist!"' After chanting the incantation three times, the priest is to rub a mixture of beer, a certain plant, and oil on the tooth of the patient.[14]

An example of another series of incantations was prepared for the victims of some disease which has been translated 'fever.' The text begins:

> Fever, unto the man, against his head, hath drawn nigh;
> Disease, unto the man, against his life, hath drawn nigh;
> An evil Spirit against his neck hath drawn nigh;
> An evil Demon against his breast hath drawn nigh;
> An evil Ghost against his belly hath drawn nigh;
> An evil Devil against his hand hath drawn nigh;
> An evil God against his foot hath drawn nigh;
> These seven together have seized upon him;
> His body like a consuming fire they devour (?).

The instructions for the cure are rather involved. A white kid is taken and placed facing the sick man. Its heart is removed and placed in the sick man's hand. A special incantation is then said, and the kid is used in sacrifice to make atonement for the man, evidently in the sense of substitution.[15] A censer and torch are used, a bandage bound on the man, and the great gods invoked: 'Invoke the great gods that the evil Spirit, the evil Demon, evil Ghost, Hag-demon, Ghoul, Fever, or heavy sickness, which is in the body of the man, may be removed and go forth from the house! May a kindly Spirit, a kindly Genius be present! O evil Spirit! O evil Demon! O evil Ghost!

[14] R. C. Thompson, *The Devils and Evil Spirits of Babylonia*, Vol. I (London, 1903), pp. LXIII ff.

[15] So R. C. Thompson, *Semitic Magic* (London, 1908), Chap. IV.

O Hag-demon! O Ghoul! O sickness of the heart! O Heartache! O Headache! O Toothache! O Pestilence! O grievous Fever! By Heaven and Earth may ye be exorcised!'[16]

R. Campbell Thompson presents this description of the work of the Babylonian priestly expert in magic:

> He was capable of defying hostile demons or summoning friendly spirits, of driving out disease or casting spells, of making amulets to guard the credulous who came to him. Furthermore, he had a certain stock-in-trade of tricks which were a steady source of revenue. Lovesick youths and maidens always hoped for some result from his philtres or love-charms; at the demand of jealousy, he was ever ready to put hatred between husband and wife; and for such as had not the pluck or skill even to use a dagger on a dark night, his little effigies, pierced with pins, would bring death to a rival. He was at once a physician and wonder-worker for such as would pay him fee.[17]

The typical attitude of the Old Testament toward this sort of thing is clearly expressed by Second Isaiah in his oracle against Babylon:

> Stand fast in thine incantations,
> In the multitude of thine enchantments
> In which thou hast toiled from thy youth!
> Perhaps thou mayest succeed;
> Perhaps thou mayest terrify!
> Thou art wearied in the multitude of thy counsels;
> Let them stand now and save thee,
> Those who divide the heavens,
> Who gaze at the stars
> Who make known by the new moons
> What things shall come upon thee.
> Behold, they are like stubble;
> Fire consumes them;
> They cannot save their lives
> From the hand of the flame. . . .

[16] Tablet XI of the *Ashakki* series: R. C. Thompson, *Devils and Evil Spirits* . . ., Vol. II (London, 1904), pp. 28 ff.

[17] *Semitic Magic*, p. lxi.

So shall they be to thee, those for whom thou hast toiled,
Thy hucksters from thy youth.
They wander about, each his own way;
There is none to save thee! (Isa. 47.12-15.)

Old Testament law is very explicit about magic and divination. The so-called Holiness 'code' (Lev. 17-26), not in itself actually a code but a homilectical explanation and expansion of older laws,[18] says: 'Ye shall not walk in the manners of the nation, which I (Yahweh) cast out before you; for they committed all these things, and therefore I abhorred them.' Consequently, everyone 'that turneth after spiritualists and diviners [literally "knowers of occult things"] . . ., I set my face against that soul.' 'A man or a woman who is a spiritualist or diviner shall surely be put to death' (Lev. 20.6, 23, 27).[19] Earlier, the Book of the Covenant places a similar ban on the female diviner or sorceress (Ex. 22.18, Heb. v. 17).

It is the eighteenth chapter of Deuteronomy, however, which gives the clearest elaboration of the old law and the reasons for it:

> When thou art come into the land which the Lord thy God giveth thee, thou shalt not learn to do after the abominations of those nations. There shall not be found among you anyone that maketh his son or his daughter to pass through fire, a diviner, a soothsayer, a magician, a sorcerer, a conjurer of spells, a spiritualist, an augur, or a necromancer. For all that do these things are an abomination unto the Lord. . . . For these nations, which thou art to dispossess, hearken unto soothsayers and diviners; but as for thee, the Lord thy God hath not suffered thee so to do. A prophet will the Lord thy God raise up unto thee, from the midst of thee, of thy brethren, like unto me; unto him ye shall hearken. (Deut. 18.9-15.)

We imply from this that the whole pagan world of magic

[16] Cf. G. von Rad, *Deuteronomium-Studien* (Göttingen, 1947), pp. 16 ff.

[19] The short apodictic form of the law in v. 27 indicates that it is an old injunction, far earlier than H (cf. von Rad, *ibid.*). V. 6, on the other hand, is homiletical expansion or reworking.

and divination is simply incompatible with the worship of Yahweh. He will make known his will when, where, and how he chooses. He cannot be tricked or coerced into revelation. He will make himself known, not by the hidden world of the occult, but by the means which he himself chooses. His word will be heard directly, clearly, and understandably through his prophet whom he sends and to whom he has revealed his counsel.

The laws against divination would have had no reason for existence, however, unless the pagan practice were known in Israel. The prophets associated it with idolatry to which the mass of the people were all too prone. During the Assyrian peril Isaiah derides the people who seek out the spiritualists and diviners 'that chirp and that mutter,' when they should seek God's direct revelation. Consequently, when in trouble they look to heaven and earth, they shall behold nothing but darkness and distress (Isa. 8.19-22). Manasseh, in the seventh century permitted and practised each of the occult arts which Deut. 18 lists as forbidden (2 Chron. 33.6). Jeremiah warns the people of Jerusalem not to hearken to their prophets, diviners, dreamers, soothsayers or magicians who say 'Ye shall not serve the king of Babylon,' for they prophesy a lie unto you, to remove you far from your land' (Jer. 27.9-10). Ezekiel says that women who prophesy by means of divination make the people to believe lies, but God will deliver the people from their hand (Ezek. 13.17-23).

The surprising thing is not that the cult of magic and divination was known in Israel, but that it should be so definitely forbidden in the law and associated by the prophets with an idolatry which destroyed rather than saved. That the power and knowledge of the God of Israel could in any way be gained by spiritualism, necromancy, astrology, or any form of the occult, seemed to the heroes of the faith as a completely incongruous idea. So perfectly clear is the Old Testament on this point that it seems strange to me its resources together with those of the New Testament are not more vigorously used by the modern Church to combat our modern superstitions which ultimately go back to the same pagan environment as that of Israel.

That does not mean to say, however, that official Yahwism was completely lacking in what we would consider magical practices or things verging closely thereon. Israel shared in the common separation of things clean and unclean. Such laws as those concerned with purification after leprosy, combining an atonement ritual with practical observation and treatment, remind one strongly of Babylonian practice (Lev. 14), as do other injunctions concerning cleansing after the violation of a tabu (e.g. Lev. 15). Dreams were regarded as important sources of revelation (cf. Gen. 40-41; Num. 12.6, etc.). The power of the word in curses and blessings was commonly recognized. The rod of Moses was evidently a magical device, for Egyptian magicians could duplicate many of its feats (Ex. 7-8). The Old Testament contains one example of trial by ordeal, that of a woman suspected of adultery, though it was a mild ordeal and one may doubt whether the woman could be harmed physically thereby (Num. 5.11-31).[20] Saul inquired of the witch of Endor, who conjured up the ghost of Samuel for him. But the reason he did so is carefully explained: 'When Saul inquired of Yahweh, Yahweh answered him not, neither by dreams, nor by Urim, nor by prophets' (1 Sam. 28.6). In other words, Saul's act was felt to be a terrible thing, an act of desperation on the part of a sinful man, who should have used other means to reconcile himself to the will of God. The mention of Urim, however, recalls the use made of the sacred dice by the priest in the early days. David frequently enquired of Yahweh by Urim and Thummim; the kind of question asked was that which could be answered by a simple 'yes' or

[20] Cf. J. Morgenstern, 'Trial by Ordeal Among the Semites and in Ancient Israel,' *Hebrew Union College Jubilee Volume* (Cincinnati, 1925), pp. 113 ff.

'no' reply (cf. Deut. 32.8; 1 Sam. 23.9-12, 30.7-8; 2 Sam. 2.1). There is no reference to the practice after the time of David; it probably was little used in subsequent ages. Closely related, if not identical, was the effort to determine God's choice by the casting of lots (e.g. 1 Sam. 19.17-24, 14.36-45; Jonah 1.7).

Furthermore, an early source pictures Samuel as a type of seer who for a fee could tell Saul the whereabouts of his father's asses. The narrative pauses to make this interesting antiquarian remark: 'Beforetime in Israel, when a man went to enquire of God, thus he spake: "Come and let us go to the seer;" for he that is now called a 'prophet' was beforetime called a 'seer'' (1 Sam. 9.9).[21] Indeed, throughout the history of Israel the problem of disentangling true prophecy from a pagan type of divination was acute (cf. 1 Kings 22; Jer. 23.9 ff.; Ezek. 13). In the eyes of Israel's great prophets the majority of those who called themselves prophets actually drew their messages from each other and from the people, not from God. For this reason Jeremiah classed the prophets of his day with the diviners, soothsayers and magicians, all of them prophesying lies (Jer. 27.9-10).[22]

S. Mowinckel and A. Guillaume have pointed to some of the penitential Psalms as evidence for a belief in the efficacy of magic, even by those who obeyed the legal prohibitions against practising it. Certain of the Psalms, they believe, were composed as prayers to God, comparable to some of the Babylonian prayers, the purpose of which was to ward off the evil effects

[21] For an excellent analysis of the significance of this passage, see A. R. Johnson, *The Cultic Prophet in Ancient Israel* (Cardiff, 1944), pp. 11 ff.

[22] For succinct treatments of Hebrew prophecy, see especially H. H. Rowley, 'The Nature of Prophecy in the Light of Recent Study,' *Harvard Theological Review,* Vol. 38 (1945), pp. 1 ff.; *The Re-discovery of the Old Testament* (London, 1945 and Philadelphia, 1946), Chap. VI; and N. H. Porteous, 'Prophecy,' in H. Wheeler Robinson, ed., *Record and Revelation* (Oxford, 1938), pp. 216 ff.

of the mysterious world of the occult.[23] While Mowinckel in particular seems to carry the argument much too far, such a Psalm as the familiar ninety-first appears to contain some evidence in favor of the general position: 'Thou shalt not be afraid for the terror by night, nor for the arrow that flieth by day, nor for the pestilence that walketh in darkness, nor for the destruction that wasteth at noon-day.' (vv. 5-6). Psalm 57 is interpreted as the prayer of a man who is caught by the incantations of enemies whose 'teeth are lance and arrows; their tongue is a sharp sword.' The Psalmist thus lies 'in the midst of lions who bewitch the children of men.'[24] The imprecatory Psalms are believed to have had a prophylactic purpose. Born of fear rather than hate, they were 'weapons of defense launched into the void to slay the sorcerer as he is at his evil work. But only Yahweh can make these anti-magical weapons effective.'[25]

In spite of the attractive nature of this hypothesis one can only say that at best it is a mere possibility. Other scholars are able to take the same Psalms and read them as cultic liturgy for a yearly festival in which the king acts the part of God who at creation slew his primordial enemies. The poems have a historical cast to their presentations, and are yet of such general nature that it is possible to interpret them in various ways and still not be sure of their precise original intent. On the surface they sound neither like prophylactics against incantations nor like cultic liturgy used in a ceremony of sympathetic magic. Most of them are surely *literary* productions to be used in worship; in this sense they may be said to be cultic. But that they were composed primarily as ritual in magical ceremonies or as protection against the danger of magic seems highly doubtful.

[23] Mowinckel, *Psalmenstudien*, Vol. I (Kristiana, 1921); Guillaume, *op. cit.*, pp. 272 ff.

[24] Guillaume, *op. cit.*, p. 282.

[25] *Ibid.*, p. 286 n.l.

In any case, it is noteworthy that none of them ever personify the source of the Psalmist's trouble as a demon. The enemy is always described in historical terms as though a human being or beings. Sickness is not caused by a malevolent spirit, but by God himself (cf. Ps. 38). In fact, so definite is the Old Testament in its exaltation of God that all things good and bad were ascribed to him. The doctrine of Satan only gradually came into being to alleviate the difficulties inherent in this view, but even in Job Satan appears as nothing more than the tester of men who has no more independence of action than God grants to him for specific projects. The world of Satan with his powers and principalities of darkness is a development in later Judaism. Consequently, our first lengthy source of information about it is the New Testament, not the Old. The world of Satan permitted Judaism to introduce a segment of the pagan world of demonology and along with it the use of spells in exorcism.[26] The New Testament world, then, is a world of demon-possession, and cures were effected when the name of Christ was used in driving out the demons (e.g. Luke 9.1, 49), or when Jesus himself commanded a demon to come forth from a person (e.g. Luke 8.26 ff.; 9.37 ff.). Jesus' enemies could thus charge him with casting out demons, not by the power of God, but by the power of Beelzebub, the prince of demons (Luke 11.15).

In the Old Testament clear references to demons are rare. Deuteronomy 32.17, in speaking of the people's idolatry says that they sacrificed unto *shedim* (the only other occurrence is Ps. 106.37), a word used in Accadian and later Judaism for demons. Yet in this passage the poet at once denies their divinity by characterizing them as a 'no-god.' Quite different is a passage which is probably Exilic in date, Isa. 34.14. The

[26] For texts, cf. J. A. Montgomery, *Aramaic Incantation Texts from Nippur* (Philadelphia, 1913); C. H. Gordon, *The Living Past* (New York, 1913), Chap. X. See also M. Gaster, '*Charms and Amulets (Jewish)*' in James Hastings, ed., *Encyclopaedia of Religion and Ethics*; Guillaume, *op. cit.*, pp. 268 ff.

author in speaking of God's destruction of Edom says that the country will revert to a wilderness inhabited by wild animals and birds. The verse in question is translated by C. C. Torrey as follows: 'And demons (*siyim*) of the desert shall meet there with goblins (*'iyim*); the satyr (*sa'ir*) shall call to his fellow; yea, there the fiend of the storm (*lilith*) shall house, and find a secure retreat.[27] *Lilith*, the female night-demon, is well known in later Judaism as also earlier in Accadian. The other terms are obscure. Two of them (*siyim* and *se'irim*) occur in another passage, probably Exilic in date also: Isa. 13.21; and the *se'irim* are spoken of as the objects of idolatrous worship in Lev. 17.7 and 2 Chron. 11.15. Much more interesting is the ceremony on the annual Day of Atonement when a goat bearing the sins of the people is sent off in the wilderness 'for Azazel' (Lev. 16.8, 10, 26). Who this Azazel was considered to be we have no information. We can only infer that it was some sort of demon thought to live in the wilderness. The ceremony is probably an old survival from a pagan background, and Azazel survived with it, not because the mysterious being played an important role in the peoples' life, but because of its connection with the rite.

These passages virtually exhaust the subject of Old Testament demonology. They indicate that Israel achieved no abstract or reasoned position regarding the non-existence of demons, just as she was unable totally to dissociate herself from magic. Historically, it would appear impossible for her to have done so. Yet from the standpoint of the various schools of pure Yahwism, demonology with the related rites of divination and magic were chiefly considered as part and parcel of paganism. So radical was the wholehearted concentration on Yahweh and so exclusive was the demand of Yahweh that loyalty and attention be directed to him alone, that the world of lesser beings simply dropped out of conscious sight. There was no

[27] C. C. Torrey, *The Second Isaiah* (New York, 1928), p. 224, and discussion on pp. 289 ff.

room for them within the framework of covenant thought. God would make known to his people directly by his spokesmen what they needed to know; no devious means of ascertaining it were necessary or proper. When the people were afflicted or appalled by the trouble and disorder of life, by the terror of night or the destruction of noon-day, they needed only to turn in faith to God. He was their Refuge and Fortress, under whose wings they could take refuge, for he promised that if man would call upon him, he would answer him, be with him in trouble, deliver him and show him his salvation (Ps. 91).

Furthermore, the true prophet, as God's spokesman, was no soothsayer in possession of numerous ritual incantations which he could chant. He was possessed by God, and there existed between him and his Lord a fellowship of understanding and a conscious communion which lifted him above his environment. The responsible nature of his call might terrify him; yet the word of God came to him: 'Be not afraid, for I am with thee to deliver thee' (Jer. 1.8). The first requirement of the God of Israel was a holy fear or reverence; but the second was one of faith: to believe in him, to accept his promises, to act obediently in love. The man who possessed such fear and faith had nothing in the world to be afraid of, except his own sin and the sin of his people. That faith was an extraordinary thing in the ancient world. It rested on a knowledge of the Divine nature and purpose which through Christ has become the basis of our own faith.

II

A second aspect of the worship of Israel must be considered more briefly. That is the nature of the religious festivals. Behind the major festivals of the pagan world lay the conception of sympathetic magic. By imitative action man could become identified with the world powers and thus make the powers do what he wanted. In the words of Professor Thorkild Jacobsen:[28]

> It is one of the tenets of mythopoeic logic that similarity and identity merge; 'to be like' is as good as 'to be.' Therefore, by being like, by enacting the role of, a force in nature, a god, man could in the cult enter into and clothe himself with the identity of these powers, with the identity of the gods, and through his own actions, when thus identified, cause the powers involved to act as he would have them act. By identifying himself with Dumuzi, the king is Dumuzi; and similarly the priestess is Inanna—our texts clearly state this. Their marriage is the marriage of the creative powers of spring. Thus through a willed act of man is achieved a divine union wherein is the all-pervading, life-giving re-creative potency upon which depends, as our texts tell us, 'the life of all lands' and also the steady flow of days, the renewal of the new moon throughout the new year.

In Mesopotamia and in all probability also in Canaan the great cult festivals centered in the divine battle drama of creation, the marriage rite of the god of rain and vegetation with the goddess of fertility, and the drama portraying the death and revival of a god, whose slaying by the forces of destruction occasioned the summer's drought. In Mesopotamia these cult festivals were matters of state with the king, as a rule, playing the chief role in the drama. Each of them is centered in the life of nature, whose personified powers battle the watery chaos, get married and produce fertility, only to be held powerless for a season before the destructive forces of nature. In the festival rites man created anew the orderly world in the battle against chaos, and he secured the revival of nature in spring and fall.

In Mesopotamia the New Year's festival was 'the most complete expression of Mesopotamian religiosity.'[29] Elaborate

[28] *Intellectual Adventure of Ancient Man*, p. 199.

[29] H. Frankfort, *Kingship and the Gods* (Chicago, 1948), p. 313. This is the Akitu Festival, for which see *ibid.*, Chap. 22, and S. A. Pallis, *The Babylonian Akîtu Festival* (Copenhagen, 1926).

ceremonies extending over a period of twelve days have been reconstructed to some extent. They were concerned with the miracle of renewal, with the message that life rises triumphantly from death or bondage. The mock battles against the hostile and chaotic powers, the finding and liberation of the god, his resumption of power, his sacred marriage, and the determination of the destiny of society for the ensuing year, were the subjects with which the ceremonies were concerned. But the rites were not merely celebrations; they were the means by which society secured its life for the year ahead. And it was the king, the focal point of meeting between the divine and human worlds, who acted in the ceremonies for society and in its behalf.

In Israel it is most significant that we have nothing of this sort in the official festivals of normative Yahwism, at least according to the law which is preserved. There is no clear record in the Old Testament of a New Year's festival in the spring. In the fall, however, which according to the old Israelite calendar marked the beginning of the year, there is one brief mention of such an observance in the Priestly calendar of the holy days and stated offerings. On the first day of the seventh month there was to be a blowing of trumpets, a holy convocation, and a cessation from servile work (Lev. 23.23-25; Num. 29.1-6).[30] The offerings differed from those offered daily: the number of animals used was merely doubled. Consequently, Gray points out that 'the seventh new-moon festival might be, from the standpoint of P, less a New Year's festival

[30] For a discussion of the obscure reference to 'the beginning of the year' in Ezek. 40.1, see G. B. Gray, *Sacrifice in the Old Testament* (Oxford, 1925), pp. 301 f. The Near East possessed two starting points for the beginning of the solar year; one in the spring at the end of winter and the other in the fall at the beginning of the autumn rains after the summer drought. The Babylonian calendar began the year in the spring, the first month being Nisan. Consequently, in Babylon itself the Akitu Festival was celebrated at that time. In Ur and Erech, however, the celebration took place in the fall month of Tishri as well as in Nisan (so Frankfort, *Kingship and the Gods*, p. 314).

than a Sabbath festival among the new moons, as is the Sabbath festival among the days of the week, the seventh year among the years, and the year of Jubilee (after 7×7) among Sabbatical years.'[31] As for the ideas connected with the occasion, we have no clear evidence until we come to the Mishnah in much later times, where it is considered the day of judgment on all living.[32] This reminds us of the last act in the Babylonian festival, which took place on the final day of the occasion; that was the determination of the destinies for the New Year. Otherwise there is no resemblance between the rites of the two religions.

In recent years much has been written about the New Year's festival in Israel, the attempt being made to reconstruct the cultic ideas from other sources than the law, especially from the Psalms, in the light of the Babylonian ceremonies. S. Mowinckel has designated a number of the Psalms as 'Enthronement Psalms.' They have to do, he believes, with the cultic celebration on the New Year's day of the enthronement of Yahweh as King. On this occasion the participants sang among many others Psalms 8, 46, 47, 93, 96-99 in Yahweh's honor.[33] In this view virtually all the Psalms were composed for use in cultic ritual; and, once the New Year's festival was established, it was a comparatively simple matter to connect the Royal Psalms, those having to do with the human king, with the festival.[34] Thus it became possible to reconstruct the essentials of the Babylonian Akitu Festival on Israelite soil.

Far more convincing are the views of Julian Morgenstern, who begins with the late Jewish idea of the New Year's day as the day of judgment. Every year on that day, he believes,

[31] G. B. Gray, *loc. cit.*

[32] *Ibid.*, pp. 303 ff.

[33] S. Mowinckel, *Psalmenstudien* II (Kristiana, 1921). For a brief review of the point of view in English, see Fleming James, *Thirty Psalmists* (New York, 1938), pp. 78 ff., where the modified views of Gunkel are followed. (Cf. Gunkel's *Die Psalmen,* Göttingen, 1926, and *Einleitung in die Psalmen,* Göttingen, 1933; and especially Elmer A Leslie, op. cit., pp. 62 ff.

[34] See above, Chap. I, note 32; Chap. II section IV.

Israel conceived of Yahweh as being enthroned in the midst of his divine attendants, holding court and pronouncing judgment. This conception was closely associated with the coming of the first rays of sun upon the morning of the day of the fall equinox, shining through the eastern gate of the Temple. The doors of this gate were kept closed during the remainder of the year, but solemnly opened at this time that the Glory of Yahweh might enter the Temple.[35] The ceremony that Morgenstern reconstructs has at least the advantage of coherence and verisimilitude within the framework of Israelite theology; and it avoids the exaggerations of the Scandinavian school of thought with regard to the precise meaning of the festival.

Yet, when all is said and attempted, the reconstruction of an elaborate New Year's festival in Israel remains almost entirely in the realm of theory.[36] In both the early and late cultic laws

[35] See Morgenstern, 'The Mythological Background of Psalm 82,' *Hebrew Union College Annual,* Vol. XIV (1939), pp. 40 ff.; 'The Gates of Righteousness,' *ibid.,* Vol. VI (1929), pp. 1 ff.; *Amos Studies,* II, *ibid.,* Vols. XII-XIII (1937-8), pp. 1 ff.

[36] For a devastating attack on Mowinckel's theories, see now Norman H. Snaith, *The Jewish New Year Festival* (London, 1947), especially Chaps. VII and VIII. I myself am unable to be so positive in *complete* rejection of Mowinckel's theories. It is possible to argue that of course no record of the New Year's festival is found in the law of Israel, because the latter was recorded by those who were trying to re-create the wilderness period when the festival was not in existence. Consequently, we are forced to turn to other types of literature, particularly to the Psalms, some of which were certainly used in enthronement ceremonies of both the Divine and human kings. If, however, Mowinckel's views are accepted, even in modified form, it must also be pointed out that the prophets for the most part emphatically rejected the presumptions of the human king in the festival. Indeed, the whole rite was probably looked upon as a semi-pagan affair in purist circles. A vital part of the theology of kingship survived in eschatological form around the figure of the Messiah, but the care with which Ezekiel avoided the term 'king' (*meleḳ*) for the future political leader indicates a profound distrust and suspicion of the older 'royal' theology. He instead chose the term 'prince' (*nasi'*), an archaic title for a tribal leader in pre-monarchial Israel (cf. Martin Noth, *Das System der zwölf Stämme Israels,* appendix).

the primary attention is focused on those occasions evidently considered more important; namely, the three annual festivals when every male was required to appear before the Lord. Those were: (1) the Passover and the associated feast of unleavened bread in the spring; (2) the feast of the harvest or Pentecost, fifty days later; and (3) the feast of the ingathering or of booths in the fall.[37] Preceding the last mentioned was the annual Day of Atonement (Lev. 16), though this is mentioned only in the latest sources.

The setting of these festivals was evidently somewhat similar to our own Christian celebrations of Christmas and Easter. The pagan background of our holy seasons is well known, and there survive such things as Christmas trees, Christmas presents, Easter flowers, rabbits and eggs. But the pagan festivals were completely transformed in the Christian setting, so that they became commemorations of historical events.

In Israel, whatever the background of the Passover may originally have been, it has become in our earliest sources the great commemorative festival of liberation, of God's deliverance of Israel from Egypt. The other three main festivals clearly have an agricultural background. But the feast of unleavened bread was connected in early Israelite times with the Passover as part of the celebration of the Exodus. In the words of the Yahwist writer: 'And thou shalt tell thy son in that day, saying, It is because of that which Yahweh did for me when I came forth out of Egypt. And it shall be a sign unto thee upon thine hand, and for a memorial between thine eyes . . ." (Ex. 13.8-9). The Deuteronomist calls the unleavened bread 'the bread of affliction,' a reminder of the severity of life in the Exodus (Deut. 16.3).

The harvest festival or Pentecost was more difficult to his-

[37] For the Passover and feast of unleavened bread, see Ex. 12-13, 24.15, 34.18; Lev. 23.4 ff.; Num. 28.16 ff.; Deut. 16.1 ff. For the harvest and ingathering festivals, see Ex. 23.16, 34.22; Lev. 23.15 ff., 33 ff.; Num. 29.12 ff.; Deut. 16.9 ff.

toricize. It was primarily a time of rejoicing when gifts of the produce were presented to the Lord, who was the owner of the land. Yet the Deuteronomist partially succeeds when he adds: 'And thou shalt remember that thou wast a bondman in Egypt' (Deut. 16.12). The feast of ingathering in the fall became the feast of booths or tabernacles (Deut. 16.13) that all 'generations may know that I made the children of Israel to dwell in booths, when I brought them out of the land of Egypt: I am Yahweh your God' (Lev. 23.43).

The Sabbath, which to the Priestly writers was the sign or token of the Sinai Covenant (Ex. 31.12-17),[38] was also given a commemorative interpretation. In the older edition of the Decalogue in Ex. 20.8-11, the seventh day is to be observed with a cessation of all work because God rested on that day in the earth's first week, and further because he blessed and hallowed it. Deuteronomy 5.15 gives another reason: 'And thou shalt remember that thou wast a servant in the land of Egypt . . .; therefore Yahweh thy God commanded thee to keep the sabbath day.'

The new moon, marking as it did the beginning of the month and of a natural division of time, was observed as a holy day. No convocation was held, but additional sacrifices were offered (Num. 28.11-14) and trumpets blown (Num. 10.10; Ps. 81.3). From Amos 8.5 we infer also that labor was suspended. As already mentioned, the seventh new moon came under the law of Sabbath observance, and so was a special occasion and in later ages at least (if not earlier) the time of the New Year festivities. While the Sabbath and harvest festivals had a commemorative significance added to them, the new moon festivals were primarily observances of the divisions of time by the moon and no historical or commemorative significance was given them. Similarly, the Day of Atonement had no commemorative significance, since its central concern was with the sin of the nation and the atonement made for it.

[38] See Chap. II, note 33.

However, festivals added later, such as Purim and Hanukkah, were commemorative, while in the Roll of Fasting of the first or second century A.D. practically every festival listed—evidently as a supplement to Lev. 23—was given a historical background of which it was a memorial.[39]

In the Hebrew festivals, therefore, we can see a variety of *motifs*. The old agricultural festivals seemed to have preserved a note of joy and thanksgiving and one of their purposes was the offering of gifts to God, who as the owner of the land had every right to claim them. The Day of Atonement was solely concerned with the nation's sin. The new moons were celebrations marking the divisions of time, as was also the Sabbath in part, at least originally. Yet the dominant *motif* in the main festivals of spring and fall was that of historical commemoration.

In the popular celebration of the festivals during pre-exilic times, especially in that of Sabbaths and new moons, paganizing practices were evidently common. Indeed the prophets disparaged their observance (e.g. Isa. 1.13-14; Hos. 2-11; Amos 5.21). Yet nowhere, at least in official Yahwism, is there the slightest hint that the primary purpose of any Israelite festival was the re-enactment of a drama, so that by sympathetic magic, by the identification of man with Divine power, the harmonious integration of nature and society could be achieved. The whole of Israelite worship was motivated by an entirely different spirit.

For the Christian Church the most important element in the Israelite festivals was the tendency toward making them historical commemorations. Perhaps the most significant differentiation between the Israelite-Christian worship and that of all other religions is to be found at this point. In natural religion the aim of the religious festivals is to preserve and continue the harmony of the social and natural worlds. Magic, gifts, flattery, cajolery could all be used in the approach to the gods, who were the powers in nature, in order to influence and even

[39] Gray, *op. cit.*, pp. 277 ff.

coerce them to act in accordance with the human will. In the worship of the Israelite and the Christian, however, the focus of attention is on the will and acts of God, especially as revealed in historical events. The Passover and the Lord's Supper are both festivals of liberation. In them the historical events are rehearsed as a memorial to the power and grace of God. The worshipper listens to this rehearsal, joins himself by sympathetic imagination with the original participants in the events, sees and hears afresh God's word and act. He then gives thanks and praise to God for what God has done, and returning to his own situation in life he solemnly renews his covenanted vows. This combination of historical narration, participation by means of memory and imagination in the original events, illumination derived from participation expressed in praise and thanksgiving, solemn renewal of covenant as the worshipper again faces his present life—such is the spiritual process which Biblical worship entails.[40] As such it avoids the pitfalls of both magic and mysticism. And in no essential respect has it anything whatever to do with the worship of polytheism. The chief religious festivals centering in historical commemoration thus respond to the primary nature of God's revelation of himself in the history of his people.

It is rather surprising that this point has not been more emphasized. It would appear that the scholars who have studied Israelite festivals in the light of those of the polytheistic environment have shown a tendency to interpret Israel's worship too exclusively by means of that in polytheism. Those, on the other hand, who concern themselves solely with the inner

[40] This description is, of course, inadequate as a complete analysis of the Christian sacrament of the Lord's Supper, unless one's view of the meaning of that sacrament is almost completely Zwinglian. But the elaboration of such a question here would raise problems completely unreal to Israel. The purpose of this analysis is merely to suggest the first and most significant difference between the Biblical sacrament and that of polytheism. Other factors arise, but they are within the context of meaning first established in Israel, though later much elaborated and debated in the Church.

Biblical evidence have likewise failed in large part to see the true revolutionary character of Israel's response to God's redemptive acts. Comparative religion is indeed one of the most difficult of disciplines because of the necessity of balancing details within a total perspective.

III

When we attempt to deal with the sacrificial forms of Israelite worship, we are immediately beset with difficulties. The Priestly writers have written in some detail about the sacrificial rites, how they were to be performed, how the cultus was organized, etc. Yet nowhere have they presented a theology of sacrifice; that we must infer as best we can from numerous allusions. When we try to compare the rites of Israel with those in the environment, we have even more difficulty because thus far the scholars have not given much attention to the subject. There is surely sufficient material available for an illuminating study of the theology of sacrifice in Mesopotamia, but I know of no thorough examination of the subject available to the student of the Bible.

The forms of sacrifice are one of the clearest indications of the influence of the environment upon Israel.[41] The purpose of sacrifice in the ancient world was conceived in accordance with the anthropomorphic ideas of deity. In polytheism the gods, while cosmic and natural, were nevertheless felt to be akin to man in inner structure. Consequently, they responded to prayers and gifts just as would human beings. Furthermore, they lived in houses or palaces just as did kings and nobles.

[41] For treatments of Israelite sacrifice in the light of the pagan environment, cf. Gray, *op. cit.*; R. Dussaud, *Les Origines canaanéennes du sacrifice israélite* (Paris, 1921); W. R. Smith, *Lectures on the Religion of the Semites* (London, 1st edition 1889; 3rd edition 1927), Chaps. VI ff.; W. O. E. Oesterley, *Sacrifices in Ancient Israel* (London, 1937). One of the most satisfactory treatments of Israelite sacrifice still remains that of G. F. Moore in T. K. Cheyne and J. S. Black, editors, *Encyclopaedia Biblica* (New York, 1903), Vol. IV, Cols. 4183-4233.

Such dwellings were the private property of the deities; they could not be entered by the common man for religious ceremonies; the latter were held in the palace courts, except on special occasions. The cosmic deities were, of course, not confined or limited by their earthly palaces. While they 'dwelt' there, the temples were symbolic microcosms of the gods' world, filled accordingly with cosmic symbolism.[42] As such, they were the bond between heaven and earth, the place where the divine could be approached. In conception and organization the temple was a large manor house in which a god and his family lived, ministered to by a large group of servants. Sacrifice, then, was one part of the total service rendered to the god, who was felt to be in need of food, drink, clothes and servants. The daily cult was essentially the caring for the god's daily needs.[43] An account has been preserved of the daily service in a temple of Erech in southern Babylonia. Four meals were provided for the gods who 'lived' in the city: the great morning repast, the small morning repast, the great evening repast and the small evening repast. Breakfast was composed of large quantities of beer, wine, milk, bread, mutton and beef. The other meals were composed primarily of the same things in varying amounts with the addition of various delicacies, and including also birds and eggs.[44]

As far as I can observe, this conception of the deity's need for and consumption of the food and drink which were placed before him was never completely spiritualized in the ancient polytheisms. In a Canaanite text from Ras Shamra occurs this typical line: 'Keret is making a sacrifice; the king is preparing

[42] Cf. the symposium by H. H. Nelson, A. L. Oppenheim, G. E. Wright and F. V. Filson, 'The Significance of the Temple in the Ancient Near East,' *The Biblical Archaeologist*, Vol. VII (1944), Nos. 3 and 4, especially pp. 47 f., 66 f., 73 ff.

[43] T. Jacobsen in *The Intellectual Adventure of Ancient Man*, pp. 186 ff., and 'Temples, Mesopotamian,' in V. Ferm, ed. *An Encyclopedia of Religion* (New York, 1945).

[44] F. Thureau-Dangin, *Rituels accadiens* (Paris, 1921), pp. 74 ff.

a banquet.'[45] Sacrifice and banquet are thus the same thing. In another text a hero named Daniel (mentioned in Ezek. 14.14), in order to obtain a son, seeks a favor of the gods by offering them food and drink offerings for a week. The text then says: 'The gods eat the offerings; the deities drink the offerings.'[46]

In the Bible we can find little of this sort of thing. To be sure the angelic messengers to Abraham accepted his hospitality (Gen. 18), as for that matter did the risen Christ from the disciples (Luke 24.30; John 21.9 ff.). The sacrifices were carefully prepared as though they were food as in paganism, including the addition of salt, but there is never the slightest suggestion of God's eating them. The nearest we can approach such anthropomorphism is the reference to God's 'smelling the sweet savor' of the burning sacrifice. The phrase first appears in the Yahwist (J) writer's flood story (Gen. 8.21), and the words, 'sweet savor unto Yahweh,' were a common, almost technical expression in the Levitical terminology (e.g. Lev. 1.9, 13, 17; 2.2, 9, 12, etc.). In usage the original meaning had been spiritualized, and meant little more than that the offering was acceptable to God.

It is quite evident, therefore, that the reaches of anthropomorphism in Israel did not extend to the conception of God's eating of the sacrificial offerings. The whole cultus in Priestly theology was God's revelation, God's gift to Israel; as such it was a prescribed form of worship, of praise, thanksgiving, communion, and especially of atonement for sin, which God accepted when it was performed both in the proper way and with the proper attitude. That the sacrifices were somehow

[45] H. L. Ginsberg's rendering of Keret C, Cols. 1-2, lines 39-41 in his *The Legend of King Keret* (New Haven, 1946), pp. 27 and 45. Cf. also Keret B, Cols. 4-6.

[46] The text is 2 Aqht I, lines 22-24, and the translation is that of C. H. Gordon, *The Loves and Wars of Baal and Anat* (Princeton, 1943), p. 33. In 2 Aqht V Daniel entertains the craftsman of the gods and shouts to his wife: 'Give the god food and drink; serve and honor him . . .,' (*ibid.*, pp. 35 f.).

needed by God or a benefit to him is nowhere felt or expressed. Consequently, Israelite skepticism could not take the form of the extreme Dialogue of Pessimism in Mesopotamia, where among other things the author goes so far as to infer that a man might cease his libations in order that his god might feel a dependence upon him for service, prayer and many other things, and run after him, begging for his worship.[47] Furthermore, the setting is prepared for such sentiments as that expressed by the Apostle Paul: 'God that made the world . . . dwelleth not in temples made with hands; neither is he worshipped with men's hands, as though he needed anything . . .' (Acts 17.24-25). The amusing apocryphal tale in Bel and the Dragon could only arise in this soil, for it tells a story, with high satirical humor, of how Daniel exposed to the Persian king the false claim of the priests that the idols actually ate the offerings.

Even more important, however, was the increasing sense of sin in Israelite cultic life. The early festivals were marked by a joyousness which was partly displaced by the somber seriousness of the cultic rites in Ezekiel and the Priestly writings. The prophetic indictment of the nation had been validated by the successive disasters which had fallen, and as a result there was a sobering, solemn feeling of the weight of sin. The Priestly writers, no less than the prophets, emphasized the persistent and perennial sin of Israel, the conditional nature of the Covenant, and the pervasive uncleanness of the people. The tabernacling of the holy God in the people's midst was the seal of the Covenant and the fulness of felicity in Priestly theology; but holiness could not mix with uncleanness. That was the reason for the fall of the nation.

At this point we should recall that polytheism had no comparable sense of sin. Many words denoting evil acts are to be found, but none of them can be rendered 'sin' in the Biblical sense of the term. Frankfort points out that

[47] See T. Jacobsen in *Intellectual Adventure of Ancient Man*, pp. 216 ff.

The Egyptian viewed his misdeeds not as sins, but as aberrations. . . . Man is not seen in rebellion against the command of God nor does he experience the intensity and range of feelings from contrition to grace which characterize the main personages of the Old and New Testaments. By the same token the theme of God's wrath is practically unknown in Egyptian literature; for the Egyptian, in his aberrations, is not a sinner whom God rejects but an ignorant man who is disciplined and corrected.[48]

As for Mesopotamia, Frankfort concludes:

There is a tendency to overrate the similarities between the Mesopotamian and the Judeo-Christian viewpoints. It is true that the Mesopotamians lived under a divine imperative and knew themselves to fall short of what was asked of them. But they did not have 'The Law.' The will of God had not been revealed to them once and for all, nor were they sustained by the consciousness of being a 'chosen people.' They were not singled out by divine love, and the divine wrath lacked the resentment caused by ingratitude. The Mesopotamians, while they knew themselves to be subject to the decrees of the gods, had no reason to believe that these decrees were necessarily just. Hence their penitential psalms abound in confessions of guilt but ignore the sense of sin; they are vibrant with despair but not with contrition—with regret but not with repentance. . . . For a chosen people conformance with the will of God can be a source of joy. For the Mesopotamians the divine decrees merely circumscribed man's servitude. Religious exaltation fell, for them, outside the sphere of ethics; it sprang from the awareness that they lived in conformity with the rhythm of divine life.[49]

In the Priestly theology of Israel the solution to the central problem of sin was provided by God in the sacrificial cultus. The cultus was thus a means of grace, though to be effective its forms must be observed with meticulous care. The heathen, of course, also poured out blood at their altars, but their rites had no meaning. Yet in Israel God had seen fit to accept the sacrificial blood as a means of atonement. By making atonement, the breach of the covenant and the problem of sin was to the Priestly mind effectively handled.

[48] *Ancient Egyptian Religion*, pp. 73 and 77.
[49] *Kingship and the Gods*, pp. 278-279.

Yet the Israelite cultus with its mode of dealing with sin did not escape the prophetic censure any more than did the Israelite institution of kingship. The prophets resented the *ex opere operato* misuse of the sacrificial system, wherein the people could multiply their offerings and throng the religious festivals while engaging in the most flagrant social evils and idolatrous practices. Sacrifice could make no atonement for the sin of a people like this. God would not accept it; he despised it. Righteousness is his demand, not sacrifice; the proper knowledge of himself, not burnt offerings (Hos. 6.6; Amos 5.21-24). God has been wearied with the constant trampling of his courts, with the vain oblations, with the many prayers of those who stretch hands to heaven which are full of blood (Isa. 1.10-17). The requirement of God is not thousands of rams or rivers of oil, but a humble, just, and loyal bearing before him (Mic. 6.6-8). Indeed, his delight is not centered in the cultus as such at all; the sacrifices he does not despise are a broken spirit and a contrite heart (Ps. 51.16-17).

The last reference from the fifty-first Psalm shows a complete spiritualization of the term 'sacrifice' which was carried on in the New Testament and the Christian Church. It was possible because God's primary desire in the covenant was a certain personal relation or attachment centered in the realm of the spirit. This alone made true and willing obedience possible, and the cultic worship acceptable. Since this was the case, God's word to the prophets condemned the whole cultic institution without exception, because it was used to validate the people's security when the true relation which made it possible had been broken.

We should note at this point that the prophetic condemnation of both the institutions of cult and of kingship would have been completely unthinkable in a polytheistic setting. Were the polytheist to strike at them, he would have been cutting away the very ground on which he stood, leaving him entirely isolated from the divine world, alone and with no means of help. But for Israel there was the covenant in which the Divine-human encounter was central and possible apart from cultus or kingship.

There has been considerable discussion as to whether the prophets meant to do away with the sacrificial cultus entirely. Taking their words literally and at face value, one would certainly infer that they did.[50] Amos seems to imply that sacrifices and offerings were not brought before Yahweh in the wilderness and, therefore, were not necessary in his day (Chap. 5.25). Jeremiah was even more definite when he said:

> What to me (Yahweh) is incense from Sheba . . . your burnt offerings are not acceptable. . . . For I spake not unto your fathers, nor commanded them in the day that I brought them out of the land of Egypt, concerning burnt offerings or sacrifices; but this thing I commanded them, saying, 'Hearken unto my voice, and I will be your God and you will be my people.' (Chaps. 6.20, 7.22-23.)

We might easily assume from these words that 'sacrifice is no necessary term of communion between Yahweh and Israel; it does not belong to the essence of religion. And that the principle extends to the cultus in general . . . is strongly suggested by the fact that (the prophets) never demand a purified ritual, but always and exclusively the fulfilment of the ethical commands of Yahweh.'[51]

A number of more cautious scholars, however, do not believe that we should assume as much as this. The prophets were merely condemning the misuse of the cultic system, and say nothing about what they might have put in its place. In this condemnation they naturally used the language of hyperbole, though in reality they really meant to point out the important thing in worship—it was not so much this as this.[52] I suspect

[50] See most recently J. Philip Hyatt, *Prophetic Religion* (New York and Nashville, 1947), Chap. VII.

[51] John Skinner, *Prophecy and Religion* (Cambridge, 1922), p. 181.

[52] So A. Guillaume, *Prophecy and Divination*, pp. 369 ff.; cf. also H. H. Rowley, *The Re-Discovery of the Old Testament,* British edition pp. 109 ff., American edition pp. 154 ff.

the truth is that the prophets did not face the question as to what they would do if the current cultus were abolished. They were not religious legislators. They had received a word from the Lord and their duty was completed when they delivered it. That this word created an uneasiness in a few souls about the cultic system then in vogue, there is no reason to doubt. One of the clearest indications of this is contained in Psalm 50.11-14:

> I (God) will take no bullock from thy house,
> From thy folds no he-goats;
> For every beast of the forest is mine,
> The cattle on a thousand hills.
> I know every bird of the mountains,
> And the animal of the field is mine.
> If I were hungry, I would not tell thee,
> For the world is mine and the fulness thereof.
> Will I eat the flesh of bulls,
> Or drink the blood of goats?
> Offer unto God thanksgiving,
> And pay to the Most High thy vows!
> Then call upon me in the day of trouble,
> And I will deliver thee, and thou shalt glorify me.

These verses appear to go farther than do the prophets in pointing out the incongruity of offering animals to the God who owns the world with all its fulness. Consequently, it seems to envisage a purified worship in which thanksgiving, the payment of vows, and prayer were central (cf. also Ps. 51.17). Yet whatever we may say about it, the fact remains that in certain Israelite circles, small in number though they may have been, an uneasiness about the sacrificial cultus did exist. Whether they would have done away with it completely, we do not know. Perhaps the truth lies somewhere between those who say that they would have abolished it and those who say that they would not have done so. The important point, in any event, is this: Under the powerful impress of this radically new theology, they pointed to the spiritual center of worship which was more primary than the cultus and by which the latter was to be evaluated. In so doing they prepared the way for the Jewish people to continue in the faith after temple and cultus had been destroyed, and they made the Christian break with the old rites the more easy. The attitude of Jesus was quite in harmony with their point of view. He said: 'I say unto you that something greater than the temple is here. And if you had known what this meaneth, "I will have mercy and not sacrifice," you would not have condemned the guiltless' (Matt. 12.6-7).

The knowledge of the Biblical God is such that every human institution must be judged by it; there is nothing so sacred that God himself may not defile or destroy it when it is used as a substitute for a people's true security. This knowledge has been possessed by a few of his worshippers in every age, beginning with the prophets and continuing to this day. The cultic reforms of the Protestant Reformation are a clear illustration. The Biblical God, unlike the gods of the nations, destroys man's harmonious existence amidst the normal supports of nature, society and cultus. He destroys every confidence, except that which is rooted and grounded in himself alone.

We must not fail to point out in conclusion, however, that the Old Testament reached no final conclusion as to how salvation was to be achieved. That God himself would intervene dramatically and fulfil history, draw all men to himself in the new Jerusalem, re-create human nature with a new heart and a new spirit, send his Prince of Peace to rule over the new community established by an everlasting covenant—of this Israel was confident. It was the only conceivable fulfilment of God's promises. But until that happened how was life to be lived? The interval became increasingly important as God's intervention was delayed in its expected form, with the result that for Judaism eschatological hope became through centuries an increasing source of difficulty even in those periods when it burned most brightly.

During the interval all Judaism could do was to deal with the problem of obedience in the most thoroughgoing manner possible. People continued to hope for the salvation promised by God; yet they also increasingly believed that salvation might come through the strictest obedience to the law of God as it was expressly written down in the Pentateuch. In this atmosphere the spirit of prophecy dried up and rabbinical Judaism developed.

In the same atmosphere, however, the Christian movement arose. The hope of the Old Testament was seen to be fulfilled in Christ. The long-promised intervention of God had occurred. The eschatological problem was resolved by the new doctrine of the kingdom as present now in Christ, though it is yet to be consummated in all its glory. The problem of salvation was interpreted in the light of the Cross and the Resurrection. The Pauline doctrine of justification by faith, based on the Yahwist's conception of Patriarchal faith as a righteousness preceding the law (Gal. 3; Gen. 15.6), was a radical criticism of Judaism's attempt to solve the problem of life in the interval by means of the law. Led by the Spirit, the Christian must live, not in ignorance or defiance of God's essential law, but nevertheless in freedom from the bondage of a law which promised a salvation it could not by its very nature provide.

Thus again we must affirm that the Old Testament in itself is incomplete. The problems of promise and fulfilment, of righteousness and grace, of sin and forgiveness, and of faith and works are unresolved when it ends. Yet the achievement of Israel in the midst of a sea of polytheism was so dynamic and revolutionary that it is and will remain the theological basis upon which the Christian faith is established. Without it the Church has no means for interpreting the real significance of the Incarnation as the early Christians saw it; it can experience only severe difficulty in arriving at a doctrine of history and revelation; it will have little protection against the subtle perversion of the Gospel by naturalism. The New Testament, no more than the Old, can stand alone. If it is not a completion and fulfilment of the faith of Israel, then it will be a fulfilment of that which we ourselves provide—the idealism of a natural religion. Only as by adoption we become children of Abraham can we become heirs of the grace of life in Jesus Christ.

INDEX

ABRAHAM, 21, 50 ff., 112
Akitu festival, 94 ff.
Albright, W. F., 7, 12 n.5, 25 n.28, 26 n.30, 29 f., 37, 46, 55 n.15, 68 n.40, 73 n.49, 79 n.3, 80
Alt, A., 24 n.25, 26 n.30, 61, 69 n.42
Amphictyony, of early Israel, 24 n.25, 61
Amos, 48, 108
Angels, patron, 31, 35
  fallen, 32 n.39
  members of Divine assembly, 33 ff.
  in N.T., 40
Animism, 12, 16
Anthropomorphism, 25 f., 41, 104
Anu, 18, 20, 25
Assembly, of the gods in polytheism, 18, 34, 36
  Divine, in Israel, 30 ff.
Asshurbanapal, library of, 80
Astrology, 80 ff.
Atonement, Day of, 99 f.
Azazel, 92

BAAL, 18, 21 f., 25 f., 36
Babel, Tower of, 53
Baethgen, Frdr., 31 n.37
Baillie, John, 74 n.50
Balaam, 82 ff.
Balscheit, B., 59 n.26
Bamberger, Bernard J., 32 n.39
Bel and the Dragon, 105
Bentzen, Aage, 28 n.32, 65 n.37
Bright, John, 70 n.44
Burrows, Millar, 39 n.56
Buttenwieser, M., 31

CAIN, 52
Calf, golden, of Jeroboam, 26 n.30
Calvin, John, 31 n.36
Cameron, George G., 80 n.8
Canaanite religion, 13, 22, 27
Carpenter, J. E., 51 n.13, 58 n.21
Celsus, 47
Chemosh, 15, 61
Cherubim, 26 n.30
Chosen People, Israel as, 46 ff.
Christ, Jesus, 40 f., 73, 77, 91, 104, 110
  as completion of O.T., 75 f., 110 ff.
Civilization, problem of, 52 f.
Cohen, A., 31 n.36
Controversy, of God, 48
Covenant, at Sinai, 15
  background and ceremonies of, 54 ff.
  meaning of, 58 ff., 105 ff.
  patriarchal, 62 n.33
  antiquity of, 60 ff.
  with David, 64, 66
Cross, Frank M., Jr., 24 n.25, 33 n.46, 37 n.52, 63 n.33

DAICHES, S., 82 n.11
David, 54, 65 ff., 74, 88 f.
Davison, 31 n.36
Delitzsch, Franz, 31 n.36
Demons, demonology, 41 n.57, 83 ff., 91 ff.
Deuteronomy, date and nature of, 62
Development, idea of, as applied to the Bible, 9 ff.
  of Israel's theological vocabulary, 70
Divination, 81 ff.
Dodd, C. H., 71 n.46
Drama, cultic, 65, 93 ff.
Driver, S. R., 10 n.4, 24 n.26, 51 n.13, 58 n.21
Duhm, 31
Dynamism, 16

EICHRODT, W., 14 n.9, 15, 55 n.17, 59 n.24, 60 n.26, 69 n.43, 71 n.45
Eissfeldt, Otto, 58 n.21

Egypt, Egyptians, 20, 25, 44 f., 63 ff., 79, 106
El, 18, 25, 79
Election, of Israel, 14, 46 ff., 74 f.
  of the king, 64
  of the individual, 69
Engnell, I., 63 n.34, 65 n.37
Enlil, 18, 25
Eridu, temple at, 16 n.14
Erith, L. E. P., 51 n.13
Eschatology, 27 f., 45, 5[illegible], 64, 71, 110 ff.
Exodus from Egypt, significance of, 14, 20 f., 49 f.
Evolution, as a clue to Israel's faith, 9 ff.
Ezra, 56
Ezra, Ibn, 31
Ezekiel, 69, 87

Festivals, religious, 93 ff.
Filson, F. V., 7, 17 n.15, 103 n.42
Fosdick, Harry Emerson, 9, 14 n.9
Frankfort, H., 13 n.7, 20, 26 n.29, 36 n.51, 44 n.2, 63, 66 ff., 94 n.29, 95 n.30, 106
Frazer, Sir James, 12
Freedman, D. N., 33 n.46, 35

Galling, K., 50 n.9, 55 n.17
Gaster, M., 91 n.36
Gaster, T. H., 34 n.47, 63 n.34
Ginsberg, H. L., 22 n.21, 34 n.47, 59 n.25, 79 n.4, 104 n.45
God, view of, according to the evolutionary conception of O.T., 12 f.
  in Israel in contrast to the gods, 20 ff.
  the living God, 26
  as Creator, 20, 29 n.35
  jealousy of, 38
  power of, 38 f., 43 f.
  in N.T., 40
  judgment of, 45
  love of, in election, 46 ff.
  righteousness of, 50 f.
  in relation to the king, 63 f.
  not influenced by magic, 82 ff.
Goddess, 18
Gods, conception of, 17 ff.
  anthropomorphism of, 26 f.
  sentenced by Yahweh, 30 ff.
  members of Yahweh's assembly, 35 ff.
  as 'no-gods', 39
  worship of, in Israel, 43
Gordon, C. H., 21 n.20, 24 n.24, 33 n.42, 80 n.6, 91 n.26, 104 n.46
Gray, G. B., 95 n.30, 100 n.39, 102 n.41
Greece, Greeks, 20, 36, 39, 46
Gressmann, H., 14 n.9
Growth, metaphor of, as applied to the Bible, 9 ff.
Guillaume, A., 82 n.11, 83 n.13, 89, 90 n.24, 91 n.26, 108 n.52
Gunkel, H., 10 n.4, 32, 52 n., 96 n.33

Hadad, 18
Hammurabi, 67
Hehn, Johs., 3[illegible]
Hempel, J., 26 n.30
Henotheism, 12, 36 ff.
History, O.T. conception of, 68 ff.
Host of heaven, 33 ff.
Hyatt, J. Philip, 108 n.50

Ikhnaton, 38 n.
Images, prohibition of, in Israel, 23 ff.
Incantations, 83 ff.
Individualism, in Israel, 69
Integration, in polytheism, 18 f., 23, 44 ff., 63, 68
Irwin, W. A., 13 n.7, 61 n.28
Isaiah, 87
Isaiah, Second, 37, 52 f., 85

Jacobsen, T., 7, 13 n.7, 17 n.15, 18 n.16, 34 n.48, 94, 103 n.43, 104 n.47
James, Fleming, 96 n.33
Jehoiada, 56
Jeremiah, 35, 69, 87, 89, 108
Jericho, early temple at, 16 n.14
John, 40

Index

Johnson, A. R., 89 n.21
Johnson, S. E., 41, n.57
Joshua, 56
Josiah, 56
Judaism, as a completion of the O.T., 75, 110 f.
Judgment, Divine, 45, 110

King, L. W., 83 n.13
Kingship, in paganism and in Israel, 63 ff., 107 f.
Kirkpatrick, A. F., 31 n.36
Kraemer, H., 74 n.50

Law, setting of, in the covenant, 58 f., 69, 106
  king's relation to, 67 f.
  Judaism's use of, 110 f.
Leslie, E. A., 32 n.40, 66 n.37, 96 n.33
Leviathan, 25, 27
Lévy-Bruhl, L., 78 n.2
Literature, religious, of polytheism, 19
  of Israel, 28, 43, 48 f., 71 ff.
Lord's Supper, 101
Love, of God, 46

Magic, in paganism and in Israel, 78 ff.
Manasseh, 35, 87
Marduk, 36
Mari, 74
McCown, C. C., 10 n.4, 15 n.12
Mendelsohn, I., 59 n.26
Mendenhall, G. E., 74 n.51
Mesopotamia, 18, 20, 25, 63, 65 ff., 80 ff., 105 f.
Messiah, 64 f., 97 n.36
Meyer, Ed., 15 n.13
Mission, of Israel, 51 f.
Moab, covenant in, 57
Monarchotheism, 38 n.54
Monarchy, in Israel, 63 ff.
Monolatry, 37 n.54
Monotheism, problem of defining, 30 ff.
Montgomery, J. A., 91 n.26
Moore, G. F., 102 n.41
Morgenstern, J., 32 n.39, 33 n.43, 88 n.20, 96 f.
Moses, 15, 24 n.26, 29, 49, 57, 88
Mowinckel, S., 89, 90 n.23, 96
Mutation, Israel's faith as, 14 ff., 20 ff., 28
Myth, mythology, mythopoetry, 19 f.
  absence of, in Israel, 26 ff.

Nature, polytheistic conception of, 17 ff., 45 f., 67 f.
  Israel's conception of, 20 ff., 36, 68
Nelson, Harold H., 17 n.15, 103 n.42
New Year's Day Festival, 27 n.32, 65 f., 94 ff.
Noth, M., 24 n.25, 57 n.20, 61, 97 n.36

Obbink, H. Th., 26 n.30
Oesterley, W. O. E., 12 n.6, 32 n.40, 102 n.41
Oppenheim, A. L., 17 n.15, 103 n.42
Ordeal, trial by, 88
Otto, Rudolf, 10 n.3, 14

Passover, 98 ff.
Paul, 40, 60, 105, 111
Pedersen, Johs., 21 n.19, 55 n.16, 58 n.22, 64 n.35, 65 n.37
Peet, T. E., 73 n.49
Pfeiffer, R. H., 58 n.21, 61 n.28
Phythian-Adams, W. J., 54 n.14, 77 n.1
Polydemonism, 12
Polytheism, nature of, 16 ff.
  cyclical view of, 71
  revelation in, 73 ff.
  magic and demonology in, 78 ff.
Porteous, N. H., 89 n.22
Priesthood, in Israel, 68 n.40
Priestly theology, 77 n.1, 99, 102 ff.
Promise, and fulfilment, as theme of Pentateuch, 50
  of O.T. history, 71
Prophets, role of, 13, 46, 68 f., 86, 89, 93
  vs. cultus, 107 ff.
Pritchard, James B., 24 n.27

Psalms, cultic origin of, 65 f., 96
as incantations *vs.* magic, 89 ff.

von Rad, G., 52 n., 56 n.18, 58 n.21, 62, 86 n.18
Rahab, 27
Ras Shamra. *See* Ugaritic literature
Remnant, 48
Renan, Ernest, 13 n.8
Revelation, Bible as, in contrast to polytheism, 73 ff.
Rider of the clouds, epithet of Baal and Yahweh, 21
Righteousness, in O.T., 59 f.
Robinson, H. W., 33 n.41, 45 n., 50 n.9, 55 n.17
Robinson, T. H., 12 n.6
Rowe, Alan, 82 n.10
Rowley, H. H., 54 n.14, 89 n.22, 108 n.52
Royce, Josiah, 39 n.56
Rylaarsdam, J. Coert, 44 n.2

Sabbath, 63 n.33, 99
Sacraments, 97 ff.
Sacrifice, meaning of, in paganism and in Israel, 102 ff.
Satan, 91
Schmidt, Hans, 32 n.40
Serpent, brazen, 24 n.26
Servant, king as, 64
Suffering, 65
Sex, as applied to the gods, 18
but not to Yahweh, 23
Shamash, 20, 67
Shechem, covenant at, 56 f., 62
Shotwell, J. T., 72
Sin, conception of, in Israel, 70
increasing sense of, 105 ff.
absence of, in polytheism, 105 f.
Sinai, Mt., attempts to locate in Arabia, 21 n.19
Skinner, John, 10 n.4, 108 n.51
Slavery, 59 f.
Smart, James D., 9 n.2
Smith, W. R., 48, 102 n.41
Snaith, N. H., 70 n.44, 97 n.36
Social order, in polytheism and in Israel, 44 ff., 107 f.
set in grace of God, 59
relation of king to, 63 f.
Söderblom, N., 74 n.50
Stars, as members of divine assembly, 35 ff.
Stauffer, E., 46 n.5

Tabernacle, 24, 61
Talmud, as a completion of O.T., 75
Temple of Solomon, 24, 26 n.30
Temples, earliest, 16 f.
meaning of, 102 f.
Tepe Gawra, temples at, 16 n.14
Teraphim, 24 n.24
Theophany, 21 n.19, 25
Thompson, R. C., 81 n.9, 84 nn.14-15, 85
Thureau-Dangin, F., 103 n.44
Tiamat, 25
Torrey, C. C., 92 n.27

Ugaritic literature, biblical parallels in, 21 f., 33, 34 n.47, 59 n.25, 79 f., 103 f.
Urim and Thummim, 88 f.

Wallace, Howard, 27 n.32
Welch, A. C., 29 n.33, 32 n.38
Wellhausen, J., 15, 32, 60 n.60
Wilson, J. A., 13 n.7
Wisdom literature, in Israel and in Egypt, 44 n.2
Wood, H. G., 72 n.47
Worship, in polytheism and in Israel. 77 ff., 100 f.
Wright, G. Ernest, 17 n.15, 22 n.22, 25 n.28, 26 n.30, 34 n.49, 58 n.23, 62 n.32, 103 n.42

Yahwist writer, view of history, 50 ff.